# AFRICA

*Angelika Taschen*

# GREAT ESCAPES AFRICA

**THE HOTEL BOOK**

TASCHEN

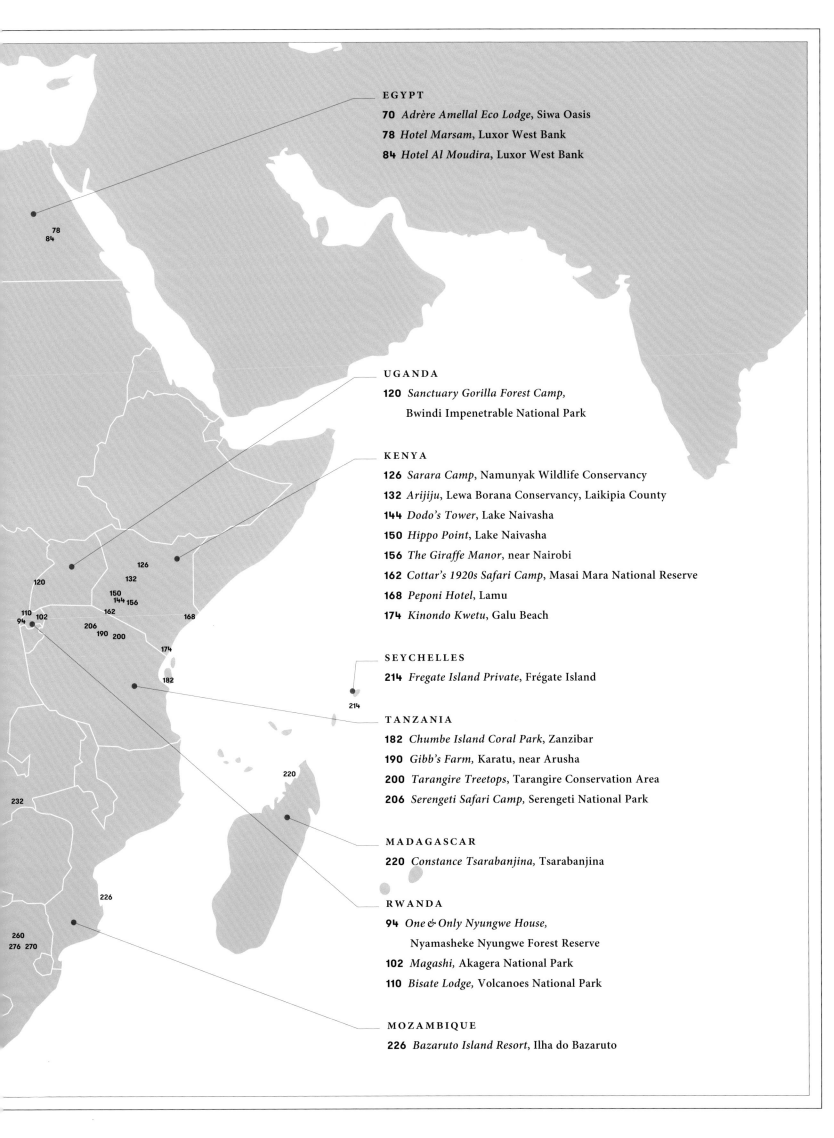

# CONTENTS

# NORD-PINUS
# TANGER

**TANGIER, MOROCCO**

# NORD-PINUS TANGER

11, Rue du Ryad Sultan Kasbah, Tangier, Morocco
Tel. +212 661 228 140 · info@nord-pinus-tanger.com
www.hotel-nord-pinus-tanger.com

## BETWEEN ORIENT AND OCCIDENT

When the Frenchwoman Anne Igou discovered this former palace of a pasha during a stroll though Tangier's Casbah, it was love at first sight. She bought the riad just a few days later and transformed it into a hotel that both gives the impression of a treasure chest and acts as a mirror of the cosmopolitan ambience and the exotic Bohemian world of Tangier. Thanks to its international reputation, in the 20th century the White City on Morocco's northern coast, once shaped by Romans, Byzantines and Arabs, and then later by the Portuguese, Spanish and British, attracted creative minds from both Europe and the United States. This is where Eugène Delacroix and Henri Matisse drew, Duke Ellington and Dizzy Gillespie played, Paul Bowles and Tennessee Williams wrote. All of them would surely have felt comfortable in the Nord-Pinus, and they would have continually had to choose a new favorite from the five guest rooms and the small house, because Anne Igou constantly changes the interior, combining antique bronze beds with modern butterfly chairs, Moroccan zellige tiles with silk from Rajasthan and colorful Middle-Eastern glass windows with black-and-white photographs by Peter Lindbergh. To prevent this eclectic mix of styles getting a little too much, there are terraces covering an area of 2,150 square feet: they offer an unhindered view into the wide blue yonder – the sky, the Atlantic and the Mediterranean, which merge together on the horizon.
◆ Book to pack: "The Sheltering Sky" by Paul Bowles.

**DIRECTIONS** *Situated at the highest point of the old town, some 12 km/ 8 miles east of Tangier Airport ·* **RATES** *€€ ·* **ROOMS** *1 room, 4 suites, plus a neighbouring house with two rooms ·* **FOOD** *In the Moroccan restaurant the "tajines" and the fish are especially recommendable ·* **HISTORY** *The riad, with a typical patio, dates from the 18th century, the hotel was opened in August 2007 ·* **X-FACTOR** *Guests are permitted to use the private beach of a nearby hotel*

# EIN MÄRCHEN ZWISCHEN ORIENT UND OKZIDENT

Es war Liebe auf den ersten Blick, als die Französin Anne Igou bei einem Spaziergang durch die Kasbah von Tanger diesen ehemaligen Palast eines Paschas entdeckte – sie kaufte den Riad nur wenige Tage später und verwandelte ihn in ein Hotel, das zugleich wie eine Schatzkiste und wie ein Spiegel des kosmopolitischen Flairs und der exotischen Boheme von Tanger wirkt. Die weiße Stadt an Marokkos Nordküste, einst geprägt von Römern, Byzantinern und Arabern sowie später von Portugiesen, Spaniern und Briten, zog im 20. Jahrhundert dank ihres internationalen Rufes kreative Köpfe aus Europa und den Staaten an. Hier zeichneten Eugène Delacroix und Henri Matisse, hier spielten Duke Ellington und Dizzy Gillespie, hier schrieben Paul Bowles und Tennessee Williams. Sie alle hätten sich im Nord-Pinus wohlgefühlt und unter den fünf Gästezimmern und dem Haus immer wieder einen neuen Lieblingsraum gewählt. Denn Anne Igou verändert das Interieur ständig, kombiniert antike Bronzebetten mit modernen Butterfly Chairs, marokkanische Zellige-Fliesen mit Seide aus Rajasthan und orientalisch bunte Glasfenster mit Schwarz-Weiß-Fotografien von Peter Lindbergh. Dafür, dass der eklektische Stilmix die Sinne nicht überfordert, sorgen die insgesamt 200 Quadratmeter großen Terrassen: Sie eröffnen den freien Blick ins Blaue – auf den Himmel, den Atlantik und das Mittelmeer, die am Horizont zusammenfließen.
◆ Buchtipp: „Himmel über der Wüste" von Paul Bowles.

ANREISE *Auf dem höchsten Punkt der Altstadt, 12 km östlich vom Flughafen Tanger gelegen* · PREIS €€ · ZIMMER *1 Zimmer, 4 Suiten; dazu ein Nachbarhaus mit 2 Zimmern* · KÜCHE *Im marokkanischen Restaurant sind die Tajine und der Fisch besonders zu empfehlen* · GESCHICHTE *Der Riad mit typischem Patio stammt aus dem 18. Jahrhundert, das Hotel wurde im August 2007 eröffnet* · X-FAKTOR *Gäste können den Privatstrand eines nahen Hotels nutzen*

# UN CONTE ENTRE L'ORIENT ET L'OCCIDENT

La Française Anne Igou eut le coup de foudre pour cette ancienne demeure d'un pacha lors d'une promenade dans la casbah de Tanger. Elle acheta le riad quelques jours plus tard et le transforma en hôtel. Le Nord-Pinus est une malle au trésor et aussi un miroir qui reflète le cosmopolitisme et la bohème exotique de Tanger. Située sur la côte nord du Maroc, la Ville Blanche qui a vu se succéder jadis les Romains, les Byzantins et les Arabes puis, plus tard, les Portugais, les Espagnols et les Anglais, attira au XXᵉ siècle des artistes de toute l'Europe et des États-Unis grâce à sa réputation internationale. Des peintres comme Eugène Delacroix et Henri Matisse, des musiciens comme Duke Ellington et Dizzy Gillespie ainsi que des écrivains comme Paul Bowles et Tennessee Williams y séjournaient régulièrement. Tous auraient aimé le Nord-Pinus et n'auraient eu que l'embarras du choix entre l'une des cinq chambres et la petite maison. Anne Igou change la décoration intérieure constamment, mariant des lits de bronze anciens avec des chaises Butterfly modernes, des zelliges marocains avec de la soie du Rajasthan et des vitraux colorés orientaux avec des photographies en noir et blanc de Peter Lindbergh. Face à ce mélange éclectique, les terrasses d'une surface de 200 mètres carrés veillent à l'apaisement des sens : elles donnent sur un bleu sans limite : le ciel, l'Atlantique et la Méditerranée ne font plus qu'un à l'horizon.
◆ À lire : « Un thé au Sahara » de Paul Bowles.

ACCÈS *Point culminant de la vieille ville, à 12 km à l'est de l'aéroport de Tanger* · PRIX €€ · CHAMBRES *1 chambre, 4 suites, plus une maison de 2 pièces* · RESTAURATION *Au restaurant marocain, les tajines et poissons sont excellents* · HISTOIRE *Le riad avec son patio typique date du XVIIIᵉ siècle, l'hôtel a ouvert ses portes en août 2007* · LES « PLUS » *Les clients peuvent utiliser la plage privée de l'hôtel voisin*

HOTEL RESTAURANT
NORD-PINUS TANGER
RIAD SULTAN

# NUMA
# MARRAKECH

**MEDINA, MARRAKECH, MOROCCO**

# NUMA MARRAKECH

37 Derba Aarjan, Rahba Lakdima, Medina, Marrakech, Morocco
Tel. +212 808 521 050 and +212 614 563 683 · info@numamarrakech.com
www.numamarrakech.com

## MARRAKECH MILANESE

Design from Milan and Marrakech doesn't go together? Clean lines and restrained shades don't harmonize with dynamic decoration and explosive colors? On the contrary! This riad is an exemplary demonstration of how well the two styles can complement one another. Its owners, Mauro Violini and his wife Claudia, used to work in PR and fashion in Milan before they felt like making a fresh start and came to Marrakech as designers. Very close to pretty Place des Épices, they designed Numa with Italian minimalism and Moroccan atmosphere. The unusual ceiling lighting made from sheets of brass in the lobby was conceived by AntiMeridian Design Consultancy in Milan and made by local artisans in Marrakech. In a corner of the typically Moroccan patio, where two orange trees grow, the owners installed a modern fireplace with stools in brass-coloured velvet – a material that runs throughout the house like a shining golden thread. And in the six individually furnished rooms, guests find both Italian furniture and Moroccan craftwork: in one room the original elaborate plaster ceiling was carefully restored and a window of multi-coloured glass inserted. Another room was painted in fresh lime green and looks out directly onto the treetops and the pool; and the shower of a suite is adorned with hand-made local clay tiles. In their role of host, Mauro and Claudia are assisted by Moroccans – and this combination of cultures, too, works so well that the warm-hearted service gains almost more praise from guests than the wonderful design. ◆ Book to pack: "The Voices of Marrakech" by Elias Canetti.

**DIRECTIONS** *In the medina of the Rahba Lakdima quarter, 5 km/ 3 miles from Marrakech airport* · **RATES** *€€–€€€* · **ROOMS** *2 rooms and 4 suites* · **FOOD** *The breakfast is delicious and generous* · **HISTORY** *Opened in spring 2018* · **X-FACTOR** *The roof terrace with a view of the Koutoubia minaret*

## MARRAKESCH MILANESE

Design aus Mailand und Marrakesch passen nicht zusammen? Klare Linien und gedämpfte Töne vertragen sich nicht mit schwungvollen Verzierungen und explodierenden Farben? Doch! Dieser Riad ist ein Musterbeispiel dafür, wie gut sich beide Stile ergänzen können. Seine Besitzer, Mauro Violini und seine Frau Claudia, waren früher in der Mailänder PR- und Modebranche tätig, ehe sie Lust auf einen Neustart hatten und als Designer nach Marrakesch kamen. Ganz in der Nähe der hübschen Place des Épices gestalteten sie das Numa minimalistisch italienisch und atmosphärisch marokkanisch zugleich. So wurde die außergewöhnliche Deckenbeleuchtung aus Messingscheiben im Eingang von der Mailänder AntiMeridian Design Consultancy entworfen und von einem einheimischen Handwerker in Marrakesch hergestellt. Im landestypischen Patio, in dem zwei Orangenbäume stehen, installierten die Besitzer eine moderne Kaminecke, in der messingfarbene Samthocker stehen – das Material zieht sich wie ein goldglänzender Faden durchs ganze Haus. Und in den sechs individuell eingerichteten Zimmern finden sich italienische Möbel ebenso wie marokkanisches Kunsthandwerk: In einem Raum wurde die originale filigrane Stuckdecke sorgsam restauriert und ein Fenster aus mehrfarbigem Glas eingesetzt. Ein anderer wurde in frischem Limettengrün gestrichen und hat direkten Blick in die Baumkronen sowie auf den Pool; und die Dusche einer Suite zieren hier produzierte Zellige. Als Gastgeber werden Mauro und Claudia von Marokkanern unterstützt – auch diese Kombination der Kulturen ist so gelungen, dass der herzliche Service von den Gästen fast noch mehr gelobt wird als das wunderbare Design.
◆ Buchtipp: „Die Stimmen von Marrakesch" von Elias Canetti.

ANREISE *In der Medina im Viertel von Rahba Lakdima gelegen, 5 km vom Flughafen Marrakesch entfernt* · PREIS *€€–€€€* · ZIMMER *2 Zimmer und 4 Suiten* · KÜCHE *Das Frühstück ist köstlich und reichhaltig* · GESCHICHTE *Im Frühjahr 2018 eröffnet* · X-FAKTOR *Die Dachterrasse mit Blick auf das Minarett der Koutoubia-Moschee*

## MARRAKECH MILANAIS

Qui a dit que le design de Milan et celui de Marrakech n'allaient pas ensemble ? Que les lignes claires et les nuances discrètes ne s'accordaient pas avec des décorations audacieuses et des couleurs éclatantes ? Ce riad prouve qu'il n'en est rien et que les deux styles se complètent parfaitement. Ses propriétaires, Mauro Violini et son épouse Claudia, travaillaient dans le domaine des relations publiques et de la mode à Milan avant de prendre un nouveau départ et de s'installer à Marrakech pour travailler comme designers. Tout près de la jolie Place des Épices, ils ont conçu le Numa en mariant le minimalisme italien et l'atmosphère marocaine. L'extraordinaire éclairage du plafond en disques de laiton à l'entrée a été conçu par le bureau d'études AntiMeridian Design Consultancy de Milan et fabriqué par un artisan de Marrakech. Dans le patio typique où s'épanouissent deux orangers, les propriétaires ont installé un coin cheminée moderne dans lequel se dressent des tabourets de velours de couleur laiton – le matériau doré est un élément récurrent dans la maison. Et les six chambres meublées individuellement abritent des meubles italiens ainsi que de l'artisanat marocain : dans une chambre, on a soigneusement restauré le plafond original en stuc délicatement ajouré et installé une fenêtre en verre multicolore. Une autre chambre, peinte en vert limette pétillant, s'ouvre sur la cime des arbres et la piscine ; et la douche d'une suite est décorée de zelliges fabriqués ici. Les hôtes Mauro et Claudia sont épaulés par des Marocains – et cette combinaison de cultures a connu un tel succès que le service chaleureux est presque plus apprécié par les clients que le merveilleux design.
◆ À lire : « Les voix de Marrakech » d'Elias Canetti.

ACCÈS *Situé au cœur de la Médina, dans le quartier de Rahba Lakdima, à 5 km de l'aéroport de Marrakech* · PRIX *€€–€€€* · CHAMBRES *2 chambres et 4 suites* · RESTAURATION *Le petit déjeuner est délicieux et plantureux* · HISTOIRE *Ouvert au printemps 2018* · LES « PLUS » *Du toit-terrasse on peut admirer le minaret de la mosquée Koutoubia*

# AMANJENA

**NEAR MARRAKECH, MOROCCO**

# AMANJENA

Route de Ouarzazate, km 12, near Marrakech, Morocco
Tel. +212 44 403 353 · amanjena@amanresorts.com
www.amanresorts.com

## A STAR IS BORN

Can there be a mirage in an oasis? Such a stunning scene in the desert is more often than not a mere vision. This could be a film set: a Hollywood dream of a Moorish palace. But the glamorous scene is real, not an illusion. This serene place is the sumptuous Moroccan resort of Amanjena; framed by pink-tinged walls, set among palms and olive trees, with a dramatic backdrop of snow-capped mountains that glitter in the sun and turn roseate at day's end. Though it is new, it has a timeless feel. The pictures of this lavish location need few words; they show that luxury is on offer here. There is the luxury of space; of calm; of rest; and privacy. You can stay secluded within the walls of your own domain, shutting out the rest of the world, if you so choose. Each pavilion has a courtyard and dining room of its own; some have private pools. The focal point is a great pool. Termed a basin, it was traditionally used to collect water from the mountains. Here its purpose is just a decorative one. Its tranquil surface reflects the sky by day; by night, it mirrors the lights of lanterns, candles and the stars. All the vigor of Marrakech is just a short drive away, as are Berber villages and beaches. Some will give thanks that two of the best golf courses are near this peaceful paradise. ◆ Book to pack: "The Caliph's House: A Year in Casablanca" by Tahir Shah.

DIRECTIONS *A 20-minute drive north from Marrakech's Menara Airport ·* RATES *€€€€ ·* ROOMS *8 houses with 2 bedrooms each, 32 pavilions with 1 bedroom each ·* FOOD *Moroccan, European, Japanese and Italian tastes opulently catered ·* HISTORY *Opened in 2000, the first Aman resort on the African continent ·* X-FACTOR *A fabulous fantasy retreat. Back to the real world at the end*

## EIN NEUER STERN AM HIMMEL

Kann es in einer Oase eine Fata Morgana geben? Denn man könnte meinen, dass ein solch überwältigender Anblick eigentlich nichts als bloße Einbildung sein kann. Dieser Ort könnte Drehort für einen Film sein: ein Traum von einem maurischen Palast à la Hollywood. Doch dieser zauberhafte Schauplatz ist keine Illusion, sondern Wirklichkeit. Die Rede ist von dem opulenten marokkanischen Amanjena-Resort – mit rosé mellierten Wänden befindet er sich zwischen Palmen und Olivenbäumen vor einer spektakulären Kulisse von schneebedeckten Bergen, die in der Sonne glitzern und sich blutrot färben, wenn der Tag zur Neige geht. Obwohl die Anlage neu ist, scheint sie zeitlos zu sein. Die Bilder dieser üppigen Anlage sprechen für sich, sie zeigen, dass hier der Luxus zu Hause ist. Sei es der Luxus, viel Platz zu haben, der Luxus der Ruhe, der Entspannung oder der Ungestörtheit. Wer möchte, kann zurückgezogen in seinem privaten Bereich bleiben und sich vom Rest der Welt abschotten. Jeder Pavillon hat einen eigenen Hof und ein eigenes Speisezimmer, manche verfügen über Privatpools. Den Mittelpunkt bildet ein großartiges Wasserbecken. Seine Bezeichnung Bassin deutet an, dass derartige Becken traditionellerweise genutzt wurden, um das Wasser zu speichern, das aus den Bergen kam. In diesem Falle dient es jedoch ausschließlich dekorativen Zwecken. Am Tage spiegelt seine ruhige Oberfläche den Himmel wider, in der Nacht wirft sie das Licht von Laternen, Kerzen und Sternen zurück. Das pulsierende Leben in Marrakesch, Berberdörfer und Strände sind nur eine kurze Autofahrt weit entfernt. So mancher wird sich freuen, dass auch zwei der besten Golfplätze ganz in der Nähe dieses friedlichen Paradieses liegen. ◆ Buchtipp: „Im Haus des Kalifen: Ein Jahr in Casablanca" von Tahir Shah.

**ANREISE** *20 Fahrtminuten nördlich vom Flughafen Marrakesch ·* **PREIS** *€€€€ ·* **ZIMMER** *8 Häuser mit je 2 Schlafzimmern, 32 Pavillons mit je 1 Schlafzimmer ·* **KÜCHE** *Aufwendig zubereitete marokkanische, europäische, japanische und italienische Gerichte ·* **GESCHICHTE** *Der erste Aman-Resort auf dem afrikanischen Kontinent, eröffnet im Jahr 2000 ·* **X-FAKTOR** *Märchenhafter Zufluchtsort mit anschließender Rückkehr in die Wirklichkeit*

## UNE ÉTOILE EST NÉE

Les mirages existent-ils aussi dans les oasis ? Car on pourrait penser qu'une vue aussi grandiose est l'effet d'une illusion. Un tel lieu pourrait servir de décor de cinéma : un palais maure comme on en rêve à Hollywood. Non, le cadre grandiose qui s'offre à vos yeux est bien réel. Ce lieu serein, c'est la somptueuse station touristique marocaine d'Amanjena. Encadrée de murs aux tons roses, située au milieu de palmiers et d'oliviers, elle a pour spectaculaire toile de fond des montagnes enneigées qui resplendissent au soleil et se teintent de rouge sang le soir venu. L'hôtel est récent, mais il inspire un sentiment d'éternité. Les photos de cet endroit fastueux parlent d'elles-mêmes : le mot clé est ici le luxe, un luxe d'espace, de calme, de repos et d'intimité. Chaque pavillon ayant sa propre cour et sa propre salle à manger, et certains disposant même d'une piscine privée, vous pouvez rester à l'abri des murs de votre domaine et oublier le monde extérieur si vous le souhaitez. Le point central d'Amanjena est un grand bassin, traditionnellement utilisé pour recueillir l'eau des montagnes. Sa fonction est aujourd'hui décorative. Le jour, sa surface tranquille réfléchit le ciel, et la nuit, elle reflète la lumière des étoiles et celle des bougies brûlant dans les lanternes. L'effervescence et l'énergie de Marrakech ne sont qu'à quelques minutes en voiture, tout comme les villages berbères et les plages. Certains seront ravis d'apprendre que deux des meilleurs terrains de golf du monde sont à proximité de ce paisible paradis. ◆ À lire : « La maison du calife » de Tahir Shah.

**ACCÈS** *À 20 min au nord de l'aéroport de Marrakech en voiture ·* **PRIX** *€€€€ ·* **CHAMBRES** *8 maisons abritant 2 chambres à coucher, 32 pavillons avec une chambre à coucher ·* **RESTAURATION** *Succulents menus marocains, européens, japonais et italien ·* **HISTOIRE** *Ouvert en 2000, il s'agit du premier hôtel Aman du continent africain ·* **LES « PLUS »** *Retraite de rêve. Le retour à la réalité est difficile*

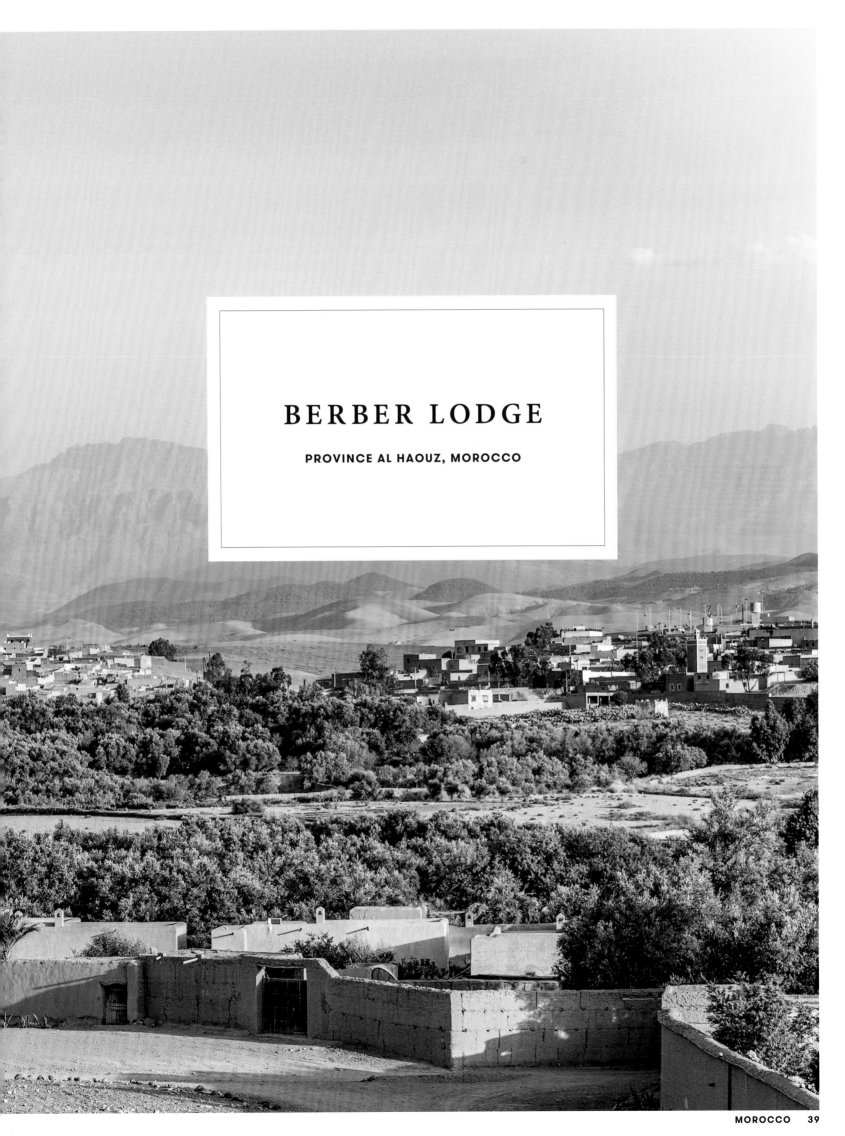

# BERBER LODGE

PROVINCE AL HAOUZ, MOROCCO

# BERBER LODGE

Douar Oumnas, Tamesloht, Province Al Haouz, Marrakech, Morocco
Tel. +212 662 04 90 54 · hotelberberlodge@gmail.com
www.berberlodge.net

## IN THE LAND OF THE BERBERS

Hidden behind a mud-brick wall in the countryside south of Marrakech, surrounded by a centuries-old olive grove, with a view of the mountains: the Berber Lodge. Inspired by the craft and building skills of the Berbers, it was constructed using their materials, including clay bricks, reeds, palm-tree trunks and eucalyptus wood. At first sight the rooms seem simple, furnished in the typical local style with woolen blankets from the Atlas Mountains and carpets from Asilah. But then guests discover luxurious accessories such as featherdown pillows, marble washbasins and even designer vintage furniture. The restrained and harmonious combination here of tradition and modernity, simplicity and exclusiveness is due to the owner's expertise and network: the Swiss interior designer Romain Michel Menière, to whom Morocco already owes such stylish addresses as the Riad Mena and the Kasbah Bab Ourika, conceived the Berber Lodge in collaboration with the Parisian studio KO, whose works include the wonderful Yves Saint Laurent Museum in Marrakech. The cuisine in this atmospheric lodge also combines the best from different ages and cultures: on plates made of Moroccan manufacture, traditional local dishes as well as modern specialties from the south of French are served, and diners have a choice between eating in the restaurant, by the jade-green pool, in the rose garden or on their own patio. ◆ Book to pack: "Wind, Sand and Stars" by Antoine de Saint-Exupéry.

DIRECTIONS *In an idyllic situation near the Berber village of Oumnas, about 40 minutes' drive south of Marrakech* · RATES *€€–€€€* · ROOMS *9 lodges, all with their own bathroom, balcony or veranda* · FOOD *Many ingredients come from the lodge's own orchard and vegetable garden, and from small regional suppliers* · HISTORY *Opened in March 2017* · X-FACTOR *The relaxed, almost family atmosphere*

# IM LAND DER BERBER

Sie versteckt sich hinter einer Lehmmauer auf dem Land südlich von Marrakesch, umgeben von einem jahrhundertealten Olivenhain und mit Blick auf die Berge: die Berber Lodge. Inspiriert von der Bau- und Handwerkskunst der Berber, wurden für ihre Häuser Lehmziegel, Schilf, Palmenstämme sowie Eukalyptusholz verwendet. Auf den ersten Blick wirken die Räume schlicht und mit Wolldecken aus dem Atlas und Teppichen aus Asilah landestypisch ausgestattet. Doch dann entdeckt man auch luxuriöse Accessoires wie Daunenkissen, Marmorwaschbecken und sogar Designer-Vintagemöbel. Dass sich Tradition und Moderne, Einfaches und Edles hier so dezent und harmonisch miteinander verbinden, liegt an Expertise und Netzwerk des Besitzers: Der Schweizer Inneneinrichter Romain Michel Menière, dem Marokko bereits so stilvolle Adressen wie den Riad Mena und die Kasbah Bab Ourika verdankt, hat die Berber Lodge gemeinsam mit dem Pariser Studio KO erdacht, zu dessen Werken das wunderbare Musée Yves Saint Laurent in Marrakesch zählt. Auch die Küche der atmosphärischen Lodge verbindet das Beste der Zeiten und Kulturen: Auf Geschirr marokkanischer Manufakturen werden überlieferte lokale Gerichte ebenso wie moderne südfranzösische Spezialitäten serviert, und man isst ganz nach Wunsch im Restaurant, am jadegrünen Pool, im Rosengarten oder auf der eigenen Terrasse. ◆ Buchtipp: „Wind, Sand und Sterne" von Antoine de Saint-Exupéry.

**ANREISE** *Idyllisch nahe des Berberdorfs Oumnas gelegen, etwa 40 Fahrtminuten südlich von Marrakesch* · **PREIS** *€€–€€€* · **ZIMMER** *9 Lodges, alle mit eigenem Bad, Balkon oder Veranda* · **KÜCHE** *Viele Zutaten stammen aus dem eigenen Obst- und Gemüsegarten sowie von kleinen Betrieben der Region* · **GESCHICHTE** *Im März 2017 eröffnet* · **X-FAKTOR** *Die entspannte, fast familiäre Atmosphäre*

# AU PAYS DES BERBÈRES

Entouré d'une oliveraie centenaire et dominant les montagnes, le Berber Lodge est dissimulé derrière un mur d'argile dans la campagne marocaine près de Marrakech. Inspirées par l'architecture et l'artisanat berbère, les maisons sont construites avec des briques de terre, des roseaux, des troncs de palmier et du bois d'eucalyptus. À première vue, les pièces semblent sobres et meublées de manière typique avec leurs couvertures en laine de l'Atlas et leurs tapis d'Asilah typiques. Et puis on découvre des accessoires luxueux tels que des coussins en duvet, des éviers en marbre et même des meubles vintage design. Si la tradition et la modernité, la simplicité et la noblesse se marient ici de manière si discrète et harmonieuse, c'est grâce au savoir-faire et au réseau du propriétaire : le décorateur d'intérieur suisse Romain Michel Menière, à qui le Maroc doit déjà des adresses aussi élégantes que le Riad Mena et la Kasbah Bab Ourika, a conçu le Berber Lodge avec le studio parisien KO, à qui l'on doit aussi le magnifique musée Yves Saint Laurent à Marrakech. La cuisine proposée ici réunit également le meilleur des différentes époques et cultures : des plats de la cuisine locale traditionnelle ainsi que des spécialités gastronomiques modernes du midi de la France sont servis dans de la vaisselle marocaine fabriquée par des manufactures marocaines, et vous pouvez manger où vous le souhaitez : au restaurant, au bord de la piscine couleur de jade, dans la roseraie ou sur votre propre terrasse. ◆ À lire : « Du vent, du sable et des étoiles : Œuvres » d'Antoine de Saint-Exupéry.

**ACCÈS** *Idéalement situé près du village berbère Oumnas, à une quarantaine de minutes en voiture au sud de Marrakech* · **PRIX** *€€–€€€* · **CHAMBRES** *9 lodges, tous avec salle de bains, balcon ou véranda* · **RESTAURATION** *De nombreux fruits et légumes proviennent du verger et du potager de l'hôtel, ainsi que de petits exploitants de la région* · **HISTOIRE** *Ouvert en mars 2017* · **LES « PLUS »** *L'ambiance détendue, presque familiale*

# SCARABEO CAMP

AGAFAY DESERT, MOROCCO

# SCARABEO CAMP

Agafay Desert, Marrakech, Morocco
Tel. +212 662 800 823 and +212 662 800 874 · info@scarabeo-camp.com
www.scarabeo-camp.com

ARRIVE. SWITCH OFF

Marrakech is a city for all the senses – and at the same time a challenge to all the senses, as you have to get used to its super-abundance of fascinating colors, textures, aromas, sounds and tastes. To get your breath back after the bustle of the medina, the perfect destination is Agafay – the stony desert that lies between Marrakech and the snow-topped peaks of the Atlas Mountains. Here Vincent T'Sas, a Belgian, and his partner Florence Mottet run the Scarabeo Camp, commanding a 360-degree view of the natural surroundings and named after the scarab beetle, which brings luck. Thanks to their original professions, he a photographer and she a graphic design, the two owners have an assured taste: the tents come in harmonious shades of white and brown, furnished simply and with items found on flea markets, as well as travel souvenirs from all over the world. The tents have private bathrooms and can even be heated in the cool winter months. There are opportunities for excursions from the camp on horseback or by camel, or to take a picnic in the mountains – but many guests simply stay on site, relax with a massage or yoga, or read the constellations in the night sky with the help of a professor of astronomy. The highlight of each day, however, is dinner by candlelight – Scarabeo is known far beyond the desert for its first-class Moroccan cooking. ◆ Book to pack: "A Child of God" by Rachida Lamrabet.

**DIRECTIONS** *35 km/22 miles south-west of Marrakech (45 minutes' drive)* · **RATES** *€€–€€€* · **ROOMS** *15 tents, including 5 family tents* · **FOOD** *Delicious, fresh local dishes – vegetarians, too, are well looked-after* · **HISTORY** *The camp opened in 2012* · **X-FACTOR** *An ideal place to relax*

# ANKOMMEN. ABSCHALTEN

Marrakesch ist eine Stadt für alle Sinne – und zugleich eine Herausforderung für alle Sinne, denn den Überfluss an faszinierenden Farben, Texturen, Gerüchen, Geräuschen und Geschmäckern muss man erst einmal verarbeiten. Für eine Atempause nach dem Trubel der Medina ist Agafay ein perfektes Ziel, die Steinwüste, die zwischen Marrakesch und den schneebedeckten Gipfeln des Atlas liegt. Hier führen der Belgier Vincent T'Sas und seine Partnerin Florence Mottet das Scarabeo Camp, eine Siedlung mit 360-Grad-Blick in die Natur, die nach dem Glückskäfer Skarabäus benannt ist. Dank ihrer ursprünglichen Berufe als Fotograf und Grafikdesignerin haben die beiden Besitzer ein stilsicheres Auge: Die Zelte sind in harmonischen Weiß- sowie Brauntönen gehalten und mit schlichten Möbeln sowie Flohmarktfunden und Reisesouvenirs aus aller Welt eingerichtet. Sie verfügen über eigene Bäder und lassen sich in den kühlen Wintermonaten sogar beheizen. Wer will, kann vom Camp aus zu einem Kamel- oder Pferderitt oder einem Picknick in den Bergen aufbrechen – viele Gäste bleiben jedoch auf dem Gelände, entspannen bei einer Massage oder beim Yoga oder lesen unter Anleitung eines Astronomie-Professors die Sternbilder des Himmels. Höhepunkt eines jeden Tages ist das Abendessen im Kerzenschein – für seine erstklassige marokkanische Küche ist Scarabeo weit über die Grenzen der Wüste hinaus bekannt. ◆ Buchtipp: „Über die Liebe und den Hass" von Rachida Lamrabet.

**ANREISE** *35 km südwestlich von Marrakesch gelegen (45 Fahrtminuten)* · **PREIS** *€€–€€€; inklusive Halbpension* · **ZIMMER** *15 Zelte, davon 5 Familienzelte* · **KÜCHE** *Feine und frische lokale Gerichte – auch für Vegetarier wird bestens gesorgt* · **GESCHICHTE** *Das Camp wurde 2012 eröffnet* · **X-FAKTOR** *Ein idealer Ort zum Entspannen*

# SE DÉCONNECTER DE TOUT !

Marrakech fait appel à nos cinq sens tout en leur posant un défi, car il leur faut d'abord assimiler l'abondance de couleurs, textures, odeurs, bruits et saveurs fascinants. Agafay, le désert de pierre qui se trouve entre Marrakech et les sommets enneigés de l'Atlas est la destination parfaite pour ceux qui désirent un peu de calme après l'agitation de la Médina. Ici, le Belge Vincent T'Sas et sa partenaire Florence Mottet dirigent le Scarabeo Camp, un campement offrant une vue panoramique sur le paysage environnant et qui porte le nom du scarabée porte-bonheur. Grâce à leur métier initial, lui est photographe, elle conceptrice graphique, les deux propriétaires ont le coup d'œil pour tout ce qui touche au style : les tentes sont décorées dans des tons harmonieux de blanc et de brun et abritent des meubles sobres ainsi que des objets trouvés dans des brocantes et des souvenirs de voyage du monde entier. Elles possèdent des salles de bains privées et peuvent même être chauffées pendant les mois d'hiver. Si vous le souhaitez, vous pouvez quitter le camp pour une promenade à dos de dromadaire ou à cheval ou pour un pique-nique dans les montagnes – mais de nombreux hôtes restent sur place et se détendent avec un massage, une séance de yoga ou observent les étoiles sous la conduite d'un professeur d'astronomie. Le point culminant de chaque journée est le dîner aux chandelles – Scarabeo est connu bien au-delà des limites du désert pour la qualité de sa gastronomie marocaine. ◆ À lire : « Zaynab, reine de Marrakech » de Zakya Daoud.

**ACCÈS** *Situé à 35 km au sud-ouest de Marrakech (45 min de voiture)* · **PRIX** *€€–€€€; demi-pension incluse* · **CHAMBRES** *15 tentes, dont 5 familiales* · **RESTAURATION** *Cuisine locale raffinée à base de produits frais – les végétariens ne sont pas oubliés* · **HISTOIRE** *Le camp a ouvert ses portes en 2012* · **LES « PLUS »** *Le lieu idéal pour se détendre*

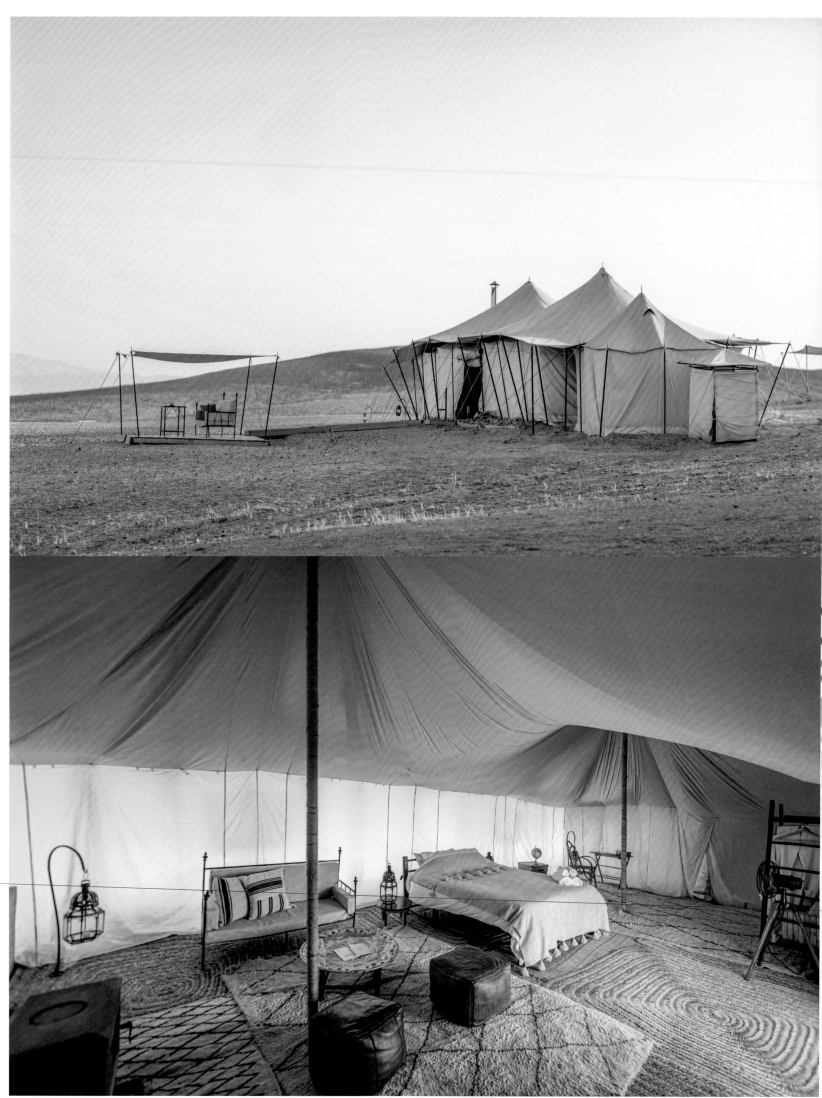

# ORIENT
# DESERT CAMP

**MERZOUGA, MOROCCO**

# ORIENT DESERT CAMP

Erg Chebbi, Merzouga, Morocco
Tel. +212 667 753 620 · orientdesertcamp@gmail.com
www.orient-desertcamp.com

## AN ORIENTAL OASIS

This camp in the middle of nowhere in the Sahara is a modern Moroccan fairy-tale: with exclusive tents, named after planets and celestial phenomena, whose wonderful beds, magnificent carpets and shining gold oriental accessories could rival any luxury hotel. In its own gourmet restaurant and a patio lit only by candles, guests sit on soft cushions after dinner, listening to the musicians and gazing into the camp fire or the glittering starry sky. Attentive staff appear discreetly from the darkness to pour out a little more tea, serve dates or conjure up delicate paintings in henna on guests' hands. The Orient Desert Camp whisks its guests away to another world – and reveals the secrets of the Sahara to them. Camel safaris head off to villages of the Gnawa, who once came from Sudan as slaves, to Lake Dayet Sri, where desert birds and flamingos live, or to the souk at Rissani, where travelers have bought supplies since time immemorial. Those who find all of this too much of a fairy-tale can book expeditions with a bigger adrenalin kick and explore the quad bike routes around the camp, try out sand surfing, or drive up and down the dunes of Erg Chebbi in a four-wheel-drive Jeep. ◆ Book to pack: "Horses of God" by Mahi Binebine.

DIRECTIONS *In the east of Morocco, 42 km/26 miles (1 hour's drive) from Erfoud, the "gateway to the Sahara". The nearest airport for domestic flights is Errachidia (70 km/45 miles from Erfoud)* · RATES *€–€€€* · ROOMS *6 tents for up to 5 persons* · FOOD *Fine Moroccan menus – with an emphasis on grilled meat* · HISTORY *Opened in December 2018* · X-FACTOR *Nomad life deluxe!*

# EINE ORIENTALISCHE OASE

Dieses Camp mitten im Nirgendwo der Sahara ist ein modernes marokkanisches Märchen: mit exklusiven Zelten, die nach Planeten und Himmelsphänomenen benannt sind und deren herrliche Betten, prachtvolle Teppiche sowie goldglänzende orientalische Accessoires jedem Luxushotel Konkurrenz machen könnten. Mit einem eigenen Gourmetrestaurant und einem nur von Kerzen beleuchteten Patio, in dem man nach dem Abendessen auf weichen Kissen ruht, Musikern lauscht und ins Lagerfeuer oder den glitzernden Sternenhimmel schaut. Und mit dienstbaren Geistern, die diskret aus der Nacht auftauchen, um noch ein bisschen Tee zu servieren, Datteln zu reichen oder filigrane Hennamalereien auf die Handflächen zu zaubern. Das Orient Desert Camp entführt seine Gäste in eine andere Welt – und verrät ihnen die Geheimnisse der Sahara. Kamelsafaris führen zu Dörfern der Gnawa, die einst als Sklaven aus dem Sudan hierherkamen, zum Dayet-Sri-See,

an dem Wüstenvögel und Flamingos leben, oder zum Souk von Rissani, wo seit jeher Reisende ihre Vorräte einkaufen. Wem das alles etwas zu märchenhaft wird, der kann auch Ausflüge mit mehr Adrenalinkick buchen und die Quadbikerouten rund ums Camp erkunden, sich im Sandsurfen versuchen oder die Dünen von Erg Chebbi im Jeep mit Allradantrieb hinauf- und hinuntertouren.
◆ Buchtipp: „Der Hofnarr" von Mahi Binebine.

**ANREISE** *Im Osten Marokkos gelegen, 42 km (1 Std. Fahrtzeit) von Erfoud entfernt, dem „Tor zur Sahara". Nächster Inlandsflughafen ist Errachidia (70 km von Erfoud)* · **PREIS** *€–€€€* · **ZIMMER** *6 Zelte für bis zu 5 Personen* · **KÜCHE** *Feine marokkanische Menüs – ein Schwerpunkt liegt auf gegrilltem Fleisch* · **GESCHICHTE** *Im Dezember 2018 eröffnet* · **X-FAKTOR** *Nomadenleben de luxe!*

# UNE OASIS AU CŒUR DU DÉSERT

Ce camp qui s'élève au milieu du désert est issu d'un conte marocain moderne avec ses tentes exclusives portant le nom de planètes et de phénomènes célestes, dont les lits splendides, les tapis magnifiques et les accessoires orientaux à l'éclat de l'or peuvent rivaliser avec ceux de n'importe quel hôtel de luxe. Il possède son propre restaurant gastronomique et un patio éclairé aux chandelles, où vous pourrez vous reposer sur des coussins douillets après le dîner, écouter des musiciens et contempler le feu de camp ou le ciel étoilé. Sans oublier les bons génies domestiques qui sortent discrètement de la nuit pour servir un peu de thé, offrir des dattes ou faire apparaître comme par magie de délicats dessins au henné sur la paume de vos mains. L'Orient Desert Camp transporte ses hôtes dans un autre monde – et leur révèle les secrets du Sahara. Les safaris à dos de dromadaire mènent aux villages des Gnaoua, originaires du Soudan et descendants d'esclaves, au lac Dayet Sri, où vivent

oiseaux du désert et flamants roses, ou au souk de Rissani, où les voyageurs ont toujours acheté leurs provisions. Ceux qui recherchent des émotions plus fortes peuvent réserver des excursions promettant des poussées d'adrénaline et explorer les routes en quad autour du camp, essayer le sandboarding ou monter et descendre les grandes dunes de l'Erg Chebbi en jeep 4×4.
◆ À lire : « Le fou du roi » de Mahi Binebine.

**ACCÈS** *Situé dans l'Est du Maroc, à 42 km (1 h de voiture) d'Erfoud, aux portes du désert. L'aéroport national le plus proche est Errachidia (à 70 km d'Erfoud)* · **PRIX** *€–€€€* · **CHAMBRES** *6 tentes pouvant abriter jusqu'à 5 personnes* · **RESTAURATION** *Cuisine marocaine raffinée qui met l'un des accents sur les grillades* · **HISTOIRE** *Ouvert en décembre 2018* · **LES « PLUS »** *La vie de nomade – dans le luxe !*

# ADRÈRE AMELLAL
# ECO LODGE

**SIWA OASIS, EGYPT**

# ADRÈRE AMELLAL
# ECO LODGE

Siwa Oasis, 18 Mansour Mohamed Street, Zamalek 11211, Cairo, Egypt
Tel. +20 2 2736 7879 · info@siwa.com
www.adrereamellal.net

## IN A SEA OF SAND

Deep in Egypt's Western Desert there is an oasis within an oasis. Nestled at the foot of the wind-sculpted White Mountain from which it takes its name, Adrère Amellal Eco Lodge is built from palm beams, salt rock and clay, a local construction technique known as "kershaf". The buildings are almost invisible in the landscape, their pale color blending into the sand. Set in acres of desert on the edge of Siwa Lake, the simple yet luxurious eco-lodge has its own date and olive orchard; a stunning swimming pool is formed around an old Roman spring. So that no electricity obscures the moon and stars, handmade candles provide the lighting, and on cold winter nights, coal-filled braziers warm the air. On the other side of the lake the Great Sand Sea, one of the world's largest dune fields, undulates towards the horizon. Ancient tombs and temples close by are testament to Siwa's long and illustrious history. It was here to the Temple of the Oracle that the Greek warrior Alexander the Great came, in 331 B.C. He sought confirmation that he was a god, more even than the extraordinary man he was. In this remote and beautiful location there is the chance for mere mortals to travel through one of the least explored deserts on earth. ◆ Book to pack: "The Alexandria Quartet" by Lawrence Durrell.

**DIRECTIONS** *Currently an 8-hour journey by air-conditioned jeep west from Cairo or 6-hour journey from Alexandria, air access planned* · **RATES** *€€€€* · **ROOMS** *42 double rooms* · **FOOD** *Egyptian and European cuisine for gourmets, most food organically grown in the lodge garden* · **HISTORY** *Egypt's first eco-lodge, opened in 1997* · **X-FACTOR** *"English Patient" territory*

## IN EINEM MEER AUS SAND

Tief im Innern der westlichen Wüste Ägyptens liegt eine Oase in einer Oase. Die Adrère Amellal Eco Lodge, ein Bauwerk aus Palmstämmen, Salzgestein und Lehm – eine für diese Gegend typische Bautechnik, die auch als „kershaf" bezeichnet wird –, schmiegt sich an den Fuß des windgegerbten White Mountain, von dem die Lodge auch ihren Namen hat. Da ihre helle Farbe der des Sandes gleicht, sind ihre Gebäude in der Landschaft beinahe nicht auszumachen. Die einfache und gleichzeitig luxuriöse Öko-Lodge, die inmitten eines riesigen Wüstengebietes am Rande des Siwa-Sees liegt, hat ihren eigenen Dattel- und Olivengarten, und ein großartiges Schwimmbecken wurde um eine alte römische Quelle gebaut. Damit kein elektrisches Licht die Mond- und Sternennächte erhellt, sorgen ausschließlich handgemachte Kerzen für Beleuchtung, und an kalten Winterabenden erwärmen glühende Kohlebecken die Luft. Auf der anderen Seite des Sees wellt sich das große Sandmeer, eine der größten Dünenlandschaften der Erde, dem Horizont entgegen. Nahe gelegene alte Grabstätten und Tempel zeugen von Siwas langer und glanzvoller Geschichte. Im Jahre 331 v. Chr. geschah es, dass der griechische Feldherr Alexander der Große hierher zum Orakeltempel kam, um sich bestätigen zu lassen, dass er nicht nur ein außergewöhnlicher Mann, sondern gar ein Gott sei. Dieser abgeschiedene und schöne Ort bietet Normalsterblichen die Gelegenheit, durch eine der am wenigsten erforschten Wüsten der Welt zu reisen. ◆ Buchtipp: „Das Alexandria-Quartett" von Lawrence Durrell.

ANREISE *Westlich von Kairo gelegen; 8-stündige Fahrt in einem klimatisierten Jeep von Kairo oder 6 Stunden von Alexandria aus, eine Fluganbindung ist geplant* · PREIS *€€€€* · ZIMMER *42 Doppelzimmer* · KÜCHE *Ägyptische und europäische Küche für Feinschmecker; ein Großteil des Gemüses stammt aus biologischem Anbau aus dem hauseigenen Garten* · GESCHICHTE *Ägyptens erste Öko-Lodge, eröffnet im Jahre 1997* · X-FAKTOR *Landschaft wie in »Der englische Patient«*

## DANS UNE MER DE SABLE

Il existe, au cœur du désert occidental égyptien, une oasis au milieu d'une oasis. Niché au pied de la Montagne Blanche sculptée par le vent dont il tire son nom, Adrère Amellal Eco Lodge a été érigé à partir de madriers de palmier, de roche saline et d'argile salifère, selon une technique de construction locale appelée « kershaf ». Les bâtiments sont ainsi presque invisibles, leur nuance pâle se fondant dans le sable. Situé au centre d'un immense désert, au bord du lac Siouah, cet hôtel écologique simple mais luxueux dispose d'un verger de dattiers et d'oliviers mais également d'une superbe piscine construite autour d'une ancienne source romaine. Afin que l'électricité ne fasse pas d'ombre à la lune et aux étoiles, des bougies faites à la main sont utilisées en guise d'éclairage et, durant les froides nuits d'hiver, des braseros réchauffent l'atmosphère. De l'autre côté du lac, l'immense mer de sable, l'un des champs de dunes les plus grands du monde, s'étend en ondulations jusqu'à l'horizon. Les tombeaux et les temples antiques voisins témoignent de la longue et glorieuse histoire de Siouah : c'est ici, dans le Temple de l'oracle, que le guerrier grec Alexandre le Grand vint chercher confirmation en 331 av. J.-C. qu'il était non pas un homme hors du commun mais bien un dieu. Ce site isolé et majestueux est l'occasion pour les simples mortels de découvrir l'un des déserts les moins explorés de la planète. ◆ À lire : « Le quatuor d'Alexandrie » de Lawrence Durrell.

ACCÈS *À 8 h à l'ouest du Caire ou 6 h d'Alexandrie en jeep climatisée. L'accès par avion est en projet* · PRIX *€€€€* · CHAMBRES *42 chambres doubles* · RESTAURATION *Cuisine gastronomique égyptienne et européenne. La plupart des produits sont cultivés biologiquement dans le jardin de l'hôtel* · HISTOIRE *Ouvert en 1997, il s'agit du premier hôtel écologique d'Égypte* · LES « PLUS » *Cadre du « Patient anglais »*

# HOTEL MARSAM

### LUXOR WEST BANK, EGYPT

# HOTEL MARSAM

Qurna, Luxor West Bank, Egypt
Tel. +20 100 342 6471 · info@marsamhotelluxor.com
www.marsamhotelluxor.com

## A PAINTERLY RETREAT

This is the place where the nobility of the country stayed. Well, if truth be told, not exactly right here, but very close – and they never left. "They" are the long dead. Preserved forever, people come here to see them in their tombs. The ancient village of Qurna, on the west bank of the Nile at Luxor, is perched on hills, their rock honeycombed with tombs. It's here in the midst of this great open-air museum that the Hotel Marsam stands. It's no wonder then that it is one of the most preferred "digs" of archaeologists. This is the closest you can get to being in ruins, by choice. Artists come here too, for the wealth of subjects. In fact, the word Marsam is Arabic for "a painter's studio." From 1941, graduate fine art students lived in part of the hotel. For the next three decades, it was like Montmartre in Paris. The art students are long gone but the hotel art gallery installed next door carries on the tradition. The simple mud brick building sits alongside waving date palms and fields of sugar cane. It is typical of the adobe style once common but now rare in Nubia and Upper Egypt. Most of the life of the hotel is centered in the lush garden, which opens to the east with a view over the fields towards the Nile and the Colossi of Memnon. The twin statues are almost all that is left of the once vast mortuary temple of Amenhotep III. ◆ Book to pack: "An Egyptian Journal" by William Golding.

**DIRECTIONS** *Beside the Ticket Office, Luxor West Bank* · **RATES** *€* · **ROOMS** *38 rooms, of which 20 are en suite* · **FOOD** *Popular Egyptian and European dishes; authentic "solar" bread served with every meal* · **HISTORY** *Some of the buildings of the hotel were built in 1920 to house archaeologists. The rest were built between 1940 and 1970 by Ali Abdul Rasoul, who was the owner of the hotel at that time* · **X-FACTOR** *Simple living in the dead center of history*

# EIN MALERISCHES VERSTECK

Hier verweilten einst die Adeligen des Landes. Um exakt zu sein, nicht genau hier, aber ganz in der Nähe – und sie haben diesen Ort niemals verlassen. „Sie" sind seit langer Zeit tot. Menschen kommen hierher, um sie in ihren Gräbern zu sehen, wo sie, für die Ewigkeit konserviert, ruhen. Das antike Dorf Qurna liegt auf Hügeln am westlichen Nilufer in Luxor – Felsgestein, bienenwabenartig mit Gräbern gespickt. Hier, in der Mitte dieses großartigen Freilichtmuseums, steht das Hotel Marsam. Dass dies eine der interessantesten Ausgrabungsstätten für Archäologen ist, überrascht daher kaum. Nirgendwo sonst kann man so nah an Ruinen (nicht am Ruin) sein wie hier. Auch Künstler kommen wegen der Fülle an Motiven hierher. Der Begriff Marsam steht im Arabischen für „Malerwerkstatt". Ab 1941 lebten Studienabsolventen der bildenden Künste in einem Teil dieses Hotels. Für die darauffolgenden drei Jahrzehnte war es das, was Montmartre für Paris ist. Zwar sind die Kunststudenten längst verschwunden, doch in der hoteleigenen Kunstgalerie, die gleich nebenan eingerichtet wurde, besteht diese Tradition fort. Das einfache Gebäude aus Lehm- und gebrannten Ziegeln grenzt an wogende Dattelpalmen und Zuckerrohrfelder und entspricht ganz dem Stil der luftgetrockneten Lehmhäuser, die in Nubien und Oberägypten einst weitverbreitet waren, nun aber sehr selten geworden sind. Das Hotelleben spielt sich hauptsächlich in dem sattgrünen Garten ab. Nach Osten hin blickt man über die Felder in Richtung Nil und Memnon-Kolosse. Die Zwillingsstatuen sind beinahe das Einzige, was von dem einst mächtigen Grabtempel Amenhoteps III. noch übrig ist. ◆ Buchtipp: „Ein ägyptisches Tagebuch. Reisen, um glücklich zu sein" von William Golding.

ANREISE *Neben dem Ticketschalter, in Luxor West Bank* · PREIS € · ZIMMER *38 Räume, davon 20 mit eigenem Bad* · KÜCHE *Bekannte ägyptische und europäische Gerichte; zu jedem Essen wird echtes „Sonnenbrot" gereicht* · GESCHICHTE *Einige Teile des Hotels wurden 1920 für die Unterbringung von Archäologen gebaut. Die übrigen errichtete Ali Abdul Rasoul, der damalige Hotelbesitzer, zwischen 1940 und 1970* · X-FAKTOR *Einfach leben, im Totenzentrum der Geschichte*

# LE REFUGE DES PEINTRES

C'est ici, ou pour être exact, tout près d'ici, que résidaient les nobles du pays. Et ils n'en sont jamais partis. Disparus depuis longtemps, préservés pour l'éternité, c'est à leurs tombeaux que l'on rend aujourd'hui visite. Le village antique de Gournah, sur la rive ouest du Nil, à Louxor, est perché sur des collines truffées de tombeaux. C'est au cœur de cet immense musée en plein air que se dresse l'hôtel Marsam. Alentour, tout n'est que ruine, par choix. Rien d'étonnant à ce que ce site soit l'un des lieux de fouilles préférés des archéologues. Les artistes y viennent également en nombre, attirés par la richesse des sujets à disposition. De fait, « Marsam » signifie « atelier de peintre » en arabe. En 1941, les étudiants diplômés des Beaux-Arts commencèrent à venir s'installer dans une partie de l'hôtel, et pendant les trois décennies suivantes, l'endroit ressemblait à Montmartre. Les étudiants en art sont partis depuis longtemps, mais la galerie d'art de l'hôtel, qui jouxte celui-ci, perpétue la tradition. L'édifice simple, construit avec des briques d'argile séchées au soleil, côtoie des dattiers et des champs de canne à sucre qui se balancent sous le vent. Ces constructions en adobe, autrefois courantes en Nubie et en Haute Égypte, y sont rares de nos jours. La plus grande partie de l'activité de l'hôtel a lieu dans son jardin luxuriant. Celui-ci s'ouvre vers l'est et offre une vue sur un paysage de champs puis, à l'horizon, sur le Nil et les Colosses de Memnon. Ces deux statues jumelles sont les uniques vestiges du vaste temple funéraire d'Amenhotep III. ◆ À lire : « Journal égyptien » de William Golding.

ACCÈS *À côté du bureau de vente de billets, rive ouest du Nil* · PRIX € · CHAMBRES *38 chambres dont 20 avec salle de bains* · RESTAURATION *Cuisine populaire égyptienne et européenne. Chaque repas est accompagné d'authentique pain « solaire »* · HISTOIRE *Certains bâtiments de l'hôtel datent des années 1920. Ils étaient destinés à accueillir les archéologues. Le reste a été construit entre les années 1940 et les années 1970 par Ali Abdul Rasoul, propriétaire de l'hôtel à l'époque* · LES « PLUS » *Vie simple au centre funéraire de l'Histoire*

# HOTEL
# AL MOUDIRA

**LUXOR WEST BANK, EGYPT**

# HOTEL
# AL MOUDIRA

Luxor West Bank, Egypt
Tel. +20 122 325 13 07 and +20 122 392 83 32 · moudirahotel@yahoo.com
www.moudira.com

## A PALACE FIT FOR CLEOPATRA

Do you fancy the life of a pharaoh? Or to live like a queen, such as the lovely Cleopatra? Of course you are too late; those dynasties are long in their tombs, but you can be a slave to luxury staying here in this modern temple. You will be given the royal treatment in a setting that is duly lavish. Al Moudira Hotel rose up on the west bank of the Nile, where the most splendid ancient sites are to be found. This latter-day palace is no more than a few minutes away from the Valley of the Kings. It was there that the most famous of the pharaohs – Seti I, Ramses II, and Tutankhamen – were laid to rest. Until they were dug up, that is, and all their grandeur revealed – then plundered. The hotel has been built on the edge of where fields end and the desert begins. Sugar cane growers tend their land just as their ancestors have done for thousands of years. In contrast to this

customary simplicity, there is this grand hotel, a work of art in a realm full of them. Its walls enclose a lush garden; the air is fragrant with jasmine and henna. Maybe these photographs might serve as a modern kind of hieroglyphics; those ancient images that showed the viewer how others lived once they could, at last, be read. So let this "dazzling mosaic" of images tell their own tale.
◆ Book to pack: "Antony and Cleopatra" by William Shakespeare.

DIRECTIONS *20 minutes from Luxor Airport* · RATES *€€* · ROOMS *54* · FOOD *Mediterranean inspired, with Levantine and oriental flavors* · HISTORY *Opened in 2002, designed by owner Zeina Aboukheir together with architect Olivier Sednaoui, and integrating pieces saved from old Egyptian buildings* · X-FACTOR *Living like Cleopatra now*

# EIN PALAST FÜR KLEOPATRA

Würden Sie gerne leben wie ein Pharao? Oder wie eine Königin, beispielsweise die bezaubernde Kleopatra? Dafür sind Sie freilich zu spät dran, längst ruhen diese Dynastien in ihren Gräbern. Aber wenn Sie sich für einen Aufenthalt in diesem modernen Tempel entscheiden sollten, können Sie einem Luxus frönen, der dem ihren gleichkommt. In einer entsprechend prachtvollen Umgebung können Sie sich wahrhaft königlich verwöhnen lassen. Das Hotel Al Moudira wurde am westlichen Nilufer errichtet, also dort, wo sich der größte Teil der spektakulären alten Sehenswürdigkeiten befindet. Dieser neuzeitliche Palast liegt nur einige Minuten vom Tal der Könige entfernt. Hier wurden Seti I., Ramses II. sowie Tutenchamun in ihre letzten Ruhestätten gelegt – zumindest bis man sie wieder ausgrub, das Geheimnis ihrer ganzen Größe aufdeckte und ihre Gräber schließlich ausplünderte. Das Hotel wurde dort errichtet, wo bewirtschaftete Felder und Wüste ineinander übergehen. Zuckerrohrbauern bestellen ihre Felder noch genauso, wie es ihre Vorfahren seit Tausenden von Jahren getan haben. Dieses Grandhotel steht in unmittelbarem Gegensatz zu einer solchen Einfachheit. Ein Kontrast, wie er hier immer üblich war. Es ist ein Kunstwerk in einem Königreich voll Kunstwerken. Seine Mauern umschließen einen üppigen Garten, und die Luft duftet nach Jasmin und Henna. Vielleicht können diese Abbildungen Ihnen ja als eine Art moderner Hieroglyphen dienen, jene altertümlichen Bilder, die dem Betrachter Aufschluss über die Lebensweise vergangener Kulturen gaben, als man sie schließlich entziffern konnte. Da es nun an mir ist, Ihnen einen Eindruck zu vermitteln, werde ich einfach dieses wundervolle Mosaik von Bildern für sich selbst sprechen lassen.
◆ Buchtipp: „Antonius und Cleopatra" von William Shakespeare.

ANREISE *20 Min. vom Flughafen Luxor* · PREIS *€€* · ZIMMER *54* · KÜCHE *Mediterran mit levantinischen und orientalischen Aromen* · GESCHICHTE *Entworfen von der Besitzerin Zeina Aboukheir und dem Architekten Olivier Sednaoui, wurde das Hotel im Jahr 2002 eröffnet; Bauteile, die aus alten ägyptischen Gebäuden stammen und erhalten werden konnten, wurden dabei integriert* · X-FAKTOR *In unserer Zeit wie Kleopatra leben*

# UN PALAIS POUR CLÉOPÂTRE

Vous rêvez de vivre la vie d'un pharaon ? Ou la vie d'une reine, peut-être, par exemple celle de la délicieuse Cléopâtre ? Bien sûr, vous arrivez un peu tard. Ces dynasties reposent depuis bien longtemps dans leurs tombeaux. Cependant, Al Moudira vous donne aujourd'hui la possibilité de faire un séjour dans le luxe d'un temple moderne et d'être traité comme un roi dans un cadre forcément fastueux. Construit au début du XXIe siècle, l'hôtel Al Moudira s'élève sur la rive ouest du Nil, où se trouvent les plus beaux sites antiques. Ce palace des temps modernes n'est qu'à quelques minutes de la Vallée des Rois où reposaient les pharaons les plus célèbres, Séti Ier, Ramsès II et Toutankhamon, jusqu'à l'exhumation et le pillage de leurs sarcophages qui révélèrent leur magnificence. L'hôtel est situé à la limite entre les champs et le désert. Les cultivateurs de canne à sucre travaillent la terre de la même manière que leurs ancêtres depuis des milliers d'années. Cette simplicité, habituelle ici, contraste avec ce grand hôtel, véritable œuvre d'art dans une contrée où on ne compte plus les merveilles. Ses murs renferment un jardin luxuriant, où jasmins et hennés embaument l'air. Nous pouvons peut-être utiliser ces photos comme un genre nouveau de hiéroglyphes, ces dessins antiques qui, une fois déchiffrés, révélèrent le mode de vie d'une autre civilisation. Laissons donc cette extraordinaire mosaïque d'images parler d'elle-même. ◆ À lire : « Antoine et Cléopâtre » de William Shakespeare.

ACCÈS *À 20 min de l'aéroport de Louxor* · PRIX *€€* · CHAMBRES *54* · RESTAURATION *D'inspiration méditerranéenne. Saveurs levantines et orientales* · HISTOIRE *Ouvert en 2002, conçu par la propriétaire Zeina Aboukheir, en collaboration avec l'architecte Olivier Sednaoui, cet hôtel réunit des objets provenant d'anciennes constructions égyptiennes* · LES « PLUS » *Vivre comme Cléopâtre à notre époque*

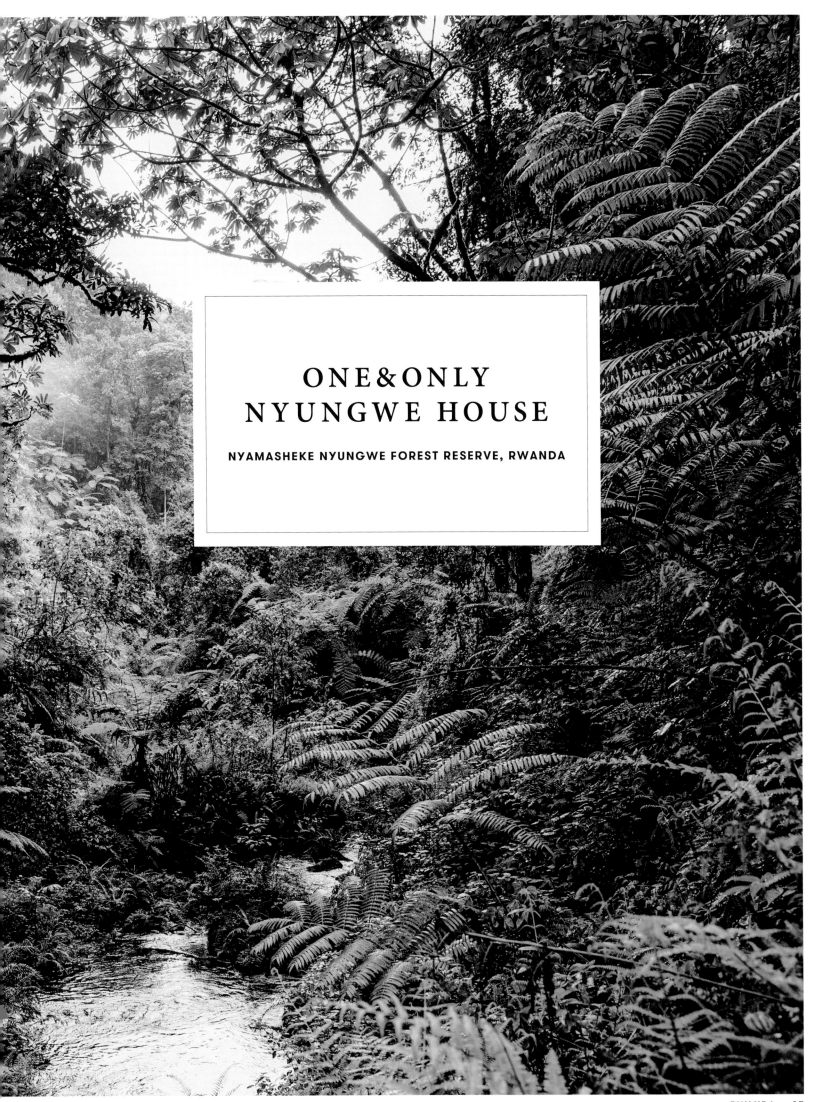

# ONE&ONLY
# NYUNGWE HOUSE

**NYAMASHEKE NYUNGWE FOREST RESERVE, RWANDA**

# ONE&ONLY NYUNGWE HOUSE

Gisakura, Nyamasheke Nyungwe Forest Reserve, Rwanda
Tel. +250 787 352 279 · info@oneandonlynyungwehouse.com
www.oneandonlyresorts.com

## GREEN SURROUNDINGS

Trees as far as the eye can see: Nyungwe National Park in the south-west of Rwanda is thought to be one of the oldest, largest and most diverse upland rain forests in Africa. It was evergreen even during the Ice Age, and today extends over a thousand square kilometers and is a habitat for rare species – from sturdy chimpanzees to delicate butterflies. It is also the country's most important source of water, the catchment area for more than two thirds of Rwanda's supply, feeding such legendary rivers as the Congo and Nile. At the margin of this unspoiled landscape, and situated so picturesquely on a tea plantation that you feel you are in the backdrop to a film, Nyungwe House welcomes its guests – with elegant rooms and suites in the African lodge style, exquisite cooking using ingredients from the house's own organic farm, and above all activities that fit the category "once in a lifetime". Whether it's a picnic with a panoramic view or a tea seminar, a course in throwing African spears or archery, trekking to monkeys or balancing on a suspension bridge at a height of 60 meters: every moment is intended to be a unique, exotic trip to a foreign world. Guests who not only want to see this world from its luxurious side, but also to support it, can help on the plantation or with work in nearby villages: the hotel is a partner of the national charity and development initiative Umuganda. ◆ Book to pack: "The Shadow of Imana" by Véronique Tadjo.

**DIRECTIONS** *230 km/145 miles from the international airport at Kigali (5 hours' drive or 30 minutes by helicopter) and 36 km/22 miles from the local airstrip at Kamembe* · **RATES** *€€€€* · **ROOMS** *19 rooms and 3 suites (which have 2 bedrooms each)* · **FOOD** *Aromatic local dishes with a modern interpretation. Don't miss the tea ceremony in the tea lounge!* · **HISTORY** *The hotel was built in 2010 with government support. Since October 2018 it has been operated by One & Only* · **X-FACTOR** *The spa with traditional African treatments*

## IM GRÜNEN

Bäume, so weit das Auge reicht: Der Nyungwe National Park im Südwesten Ruandas gilt als einer der ältesten, größten und vielfältigsten Bergregenwälder Afrikas. Selbst in der Eiszeit immergrün, dehnt er sich heute auf 1000 Quadratkilometern aus und ist Lebensraum seltener Spezies – von mächtigen Schimpansen bis zu filigranen Schmetterlingen. Zudem ist er die wichtigste Quelle des Landes: Mehr als zwei Drittel von Ruandas Wasser sammeln sich auf seinem Areal, und er speist legendäre Flüsse wie den Kongo und Nil. Am Rand dieser ursprünglichen Landschaft und so malerisch auf einer Teeplantage gelegen, dass man sich in einer Kinokulisse glaubt, empfängt das Nyungwe House seine Gäste. Mit eleganten Zimmern und Suiten im afrikanischen Lodgestil, feinster Küche mit Zutaten aus eigenem Bioanbau – und vor allem Aktivitäten, die alle nach dem Motto „einmal im Leben" zusammengestellt sind. Ob es sich um ein Picknick mit Panoramablick oder ein Teeseminar handelt, einen Kurs im afrikanischen Speerwerfen oder Bogenschießen, ein Affentrekking oder einen Balanceakt über

eine Hängebrücke in 60 Metern Höhe: Jeder Moment soll ein einzigartiger und exotischer Ausflug in eine fremde Welt sein. Wer diese Welt nicht nur von der luxuriösen Seite aus kennenlernen, sondern auch unterstützen möchte, kann auf der Plantage oder bei Arbeiten in nahen Dörfern helfen – das Hotel ist Partner der nationalen Wohltätigkeits- und Entwicklungshilfe-Initiative Umuganda. ◆ Buchtipp: „Der Schatten Gottes" von Véronique Tadjo.

**ANREISE** *230 km vom internationalen Flughafen Kigali (5 Fahrtstunden oder 30 Flugminuten im Helikopter) und 36 km vom lokalen Flugplatz Kamembe entfernt* · **PREIS** *€€€€* · **ZIMMER** *19 Zimmer und 3 Suiten (diese mit je 2 Schlafzimmern)* · **KÜCHE** *Aromatische lokale Gerichte, modern interpretiert. Nicht verpassen: die Teezeremonie in der „Tea Lounge"!* · **GESCHICHTE** *2010 wurde das Hotel mit Unterstützung der Regierung erbaut. Seit Oktober 2018 wird es von One & Only geführt* · **X-FAKTOR** *Das Spa mit traditionellen afrikanischen Anwendungen*

## EN PLEINE VERDURE

Des arbres à perte de vue : le parc national de Nyungwe, dans le sud-ouest du Rwanda, abrite l'une des plus anciennes, des plus grandes et des plus diversifiées forêts tropicales de montagne en Afrique. Restée verte même à l'époque glaciaire, elle s'étend aujourd'hui sur plus de 1 000 kilomètres carrés, un habitat pour des espèces rares – des vigoureux chimpanzés aux papillons délicats. Elle abrite aussi la source la plus importante du pays : plus des deux tiers de l'eau du Rwanda est collectée sur son territoire et alimente des fleuves mythiques tels que le Congo et le Nil. À l'orée de ce paysage vierge, et située de manière pittoresque sur une plantation de thé – on se croirait dans un décor de cinéma –, Nyungwe House accueille ses hôtes. Avec des chambres et des suites élégantes dans le style lodge africain, une cuisine raffinée à base de produits issus de l'agriculture biologique – et surtout des activités, qui sont toutes organisées selon la devise « une fois dans sa vie ». Qu'il s'agisse d'un pique-nique avec vue panoramique ou d'un séminaire sur le thé, d'un cours de tir à l'arc ou de tir au javelot africain, de randonnées à la recherche des singes ou d'un

numéro d'équilibre sur un pont suspendu à 60 mètres de hauteur : il doit s'agir chaque fois d'une excursion unique et exotique dans un monde inconnu. Ceux qui veulent non seulement connaître les aspects luxueux de ce monde, mais aussi le soutenir, peuvent travailler sur la plantation ou dans les villages voisins – l'hôtel est un partenaire de l'initiative traditionnelle des travaux d'intérêt général, l'Umuganda. ◆ À lire : « L'ombre d'Imana – Voyages jusqu'au bout du Rwanda » de Véronique Tadjo.

**ACCÈS** *Situé à 230 km de l'aéroport international de Kigali (5 h de voiture ou 30 min en hélicoptère) et à 36 km du petit aéroport de Kamembe* · **PRIX** *€€€€* · **CHAMBRES** *19 chambres et 3 suites (chacune disposant de 2 chambres à coucher)* · **RESTAURATION** *Cuisine locale savoureuse, interprétée de manière moderne. À ne pas manquer : la cérémonie du thé dans la « Tea Lounge » !* · **HISTOIRE** *L'hôtel a été construit en 2010 avec le soutien du gouvernement. Depuis octobre 2018 il est dirigé par One & Only* · **LES « PLUS »** *Le spa qui propose des soins africains traditionnels*

# MAGASHI

### AKAGERA NATIONAL PARK, RWANDA

# MAGASHI

Akagera National Park, Rwanda
Tel. +27 11 257 50 00 · enquiry@wilderness.co.za
www.wilderness-safaris.com

## SAFARIS ON THE LAKE

A delicate balance had to be maintained in the Akagera National Park in the north-east of Rwanda. When Rwandan refugees were able to return home after the civil war and appalling genocide in 1994, they had to build their livelihoods again and took advantage of the resources of nature: wood from the forests, water, fish, animals that were hunted. All of this was necessary for survival. However, though much the land came to the aid of its inhabitants, their sudden intervention brought the ecosystem of the national park to the verge of collapse. Yet the operators of the park managed this balancing act. Today Akagera provides for the lives of its residents and is also, on a more modest scale, one of the most important protected swamp areas in Africa. Here Magashi lodge has dedicated itself to preserving the flora and fauna, as well as local culture and traditions. Secluded, in green surroundings with a view of Lake Rwanyakazinga, its tents exude a typical East African safari atmosphere. Elegant and bright, they are furnished with many local items: visitors admire bamboo partitions, tiles painted with graphic patterns according to the old "imigongo" art, lamps whose design is reminiscent of the headdress of the former kings of Rwanda, and candelabras shaped like the horns of Rwandan ankole cattle. As befits a safari camp, Magashi serves an early breakfast before guests set out to watch the animals, a brunch after they return, and classic high tea in late afternoon. ◆ Book to pack: "Invictus" by John Carlin.

DIRECTIONS *In the north-east of Rwanda, close to the Tanzanian border. 110 km/68 miles from Kigali (c. 2.5 to 3 hours' drive)* · RATES *€€€€; all inclusive* · ROOMS *6 tents all with their own bathroom* · FOOD *Fresh and light, with many meals based on fruit and vegetables grown locally. Rwandan coffee and tea are also delicious* · HISTORY *Opened in spring 2019* · X-FACTOR *The national park is famous for its hippos, crocodiles and about 500 species of birds*

## SAFARIS AM SEE

Es war ein empfindliches Gleichgewicht, das sich im Akagera National Park im Nordosten Ruandas einstellen musste: Als nach dem Bürgerkrieg und grausamen Völkermord 1994 ruandische Flüchtlinge in ihre Heimat zurückkehren konnten, mussten sie ihre Existenz neu aufbauen und griffen auf die Resourcen der Natur zurück: Holz aus den Wäldern, Wasser, Fische, Wild – all das war überlebensnotwendig. Aber so sehr das Land den Bewohnern auch half, die plötzlichen Eingriffe brachten das Ökosystem des Parks zugleich an den Rand des Kollaps. Doch die Betreiber schafften den Balanceakt. Akagera ist heute Lebensraum für seine Menschen und, auf einer verkleinerten Fläche, eines der wichtigsten naturgeschützten Feuchtgebiete Afrikas. Hier hat sich auch die Magashi-Lodge der Bewahrung von Flora und Fauna sowie lokaler Kultur und Tradition verschrieben. Wie ein verwunschener Ort liegt die Lodge mitten im Grünen. Ihre Zelte mit dem typisch ostafrikanischen Safariflair blicken auf den Lake Rwanyakazinga. Elegant und lichtdurchflutet, sind sie mit vielen einheimischem Elementen eingerichtet – man bewundert Raumteiler aus Bambus, Fliesen, die nach der alten Kunst des „imigongo" mit grafischen Mustern bemalt sind, Lampen, deren Design an den Kopfschmuck der früheren Könige von Ruanda erinnert, und Kerzenständer, die wie die Hörner des ruandischen Ankolerinds geformt sind. Wie es sich für ein Safaricamp gehört, serviert Magashi ein zeitiges Frühstück, ehe die Gäste zu Tierbeobachtungen aufbrechen, einen Brunch nach ihrer Rückkehr sowie klassischen High Tea am späten Nachmittag. ◆ Buchtipp: „Ein Leben mehr" von Esther Mujawayo.

ANREISE *Im Nordosten Ruandas gelegen, nahe der Grenze zu Tansania. 110 km vom Kigali entfernt (ca. 2,5-3 Fahrtstunden)* · PREIS *€€€€; all-inclusive* · ZIMMER *6 Zelte, jeweils mit eigenem Bad* · KÜCHE *Frisch und leicht – viele Mahlzeiten basieren auf regionalem Obst und Gemüse. Auch der ruandische Kaffee und Tee sind köstlich* · GESCHICHTE *Im Frühjahr 2019 eröffnet* · X-FAKTOR *Der Nationalpark ist berühmt für seine Nilpferde, Krokodile und rund 500 Vogelarten*

## SAFARIS AU BORD DU LAC

Le Parc National de l'Akagera, dans le nord-est du Rwanda, a connu des moments difficiles : lorsque les réfugiés rwandais ont pu rentrer chez eux après la guerre civile et le génocide de 1994, ils ont dû reconstruire leur existence et puiser dans les ressources naturelles : bois des forêts, eau, poisson, gibier – tout cela était essentiel pour survivre. La terre a aidé les habitants, mais ces interventions soudaines ont amené l'écosystème du parc au bord de l'effondrement. Les opérateurs ont toutefois réussi à le faire renaître. Aujourd'hui, l'Akagera est un espace de vie pour ses habitants et, sur un espace réduit, une des zones humides protégées les plus importantes d'Afrique. Ici, le Magashi consacre également ses efforts à la préservation de la flore et de la faune ainsi que de la culture et des traditions locales. Perdues au milieu de la verdure et avec vue sur le lac Rwanyakazinga, ses tentes évoquent l'atmosphère typique d'un safari en Afrique de l'Est. Élégantes et inondées de lumière, elles sont meublées de nombreux éléments locaux – on peut admirer des cloisons de séparation en bambou, des carreaux peints de motifs géométriques selon l'art imigongo traditionnel, des lampes dont le design rappelle les coiffures des anciens rois du Rwanda, des chandeliers dont la forme évoque les cornes du watusi, le bœuf rwandais. Comme tout camp de safari qui se respecte, Magashi sert un petit-déjeuner matinal avant que les invités ne partent observer le gibier, un brunch après leur retour, et un thé classique en fin d'après-midi. ◆ À lire : « Survivantes » d'Esther Mujawayo.

ACCÈS *Situé au nord-est du Rwanda, près de la frontière tanzanienne. À 110 km de Kigali (environ 2,5 h–3 h de route)* · PRIX *€€€€; tout compris* · CHAMBRES *6 tentes avec salle de bains attenante* · RESTAURATION *Cuisine légère et fraîche – de nombreux repas sont préparés avec des légumes et des fruits cultivés sur place. Le café et le thé rwandais sont délicieux* · HISTOIRE *Existe depuis le printemps 2019* · LES « PLUS » *Le parc national est réputé pour ses hippopotames, ses crocodiles et environ 500 espèces d'oiseaux*

# BISATE LODGE

## VOLCANOES NATIONAL PARK, RWANDA

# BISATE LODGE

Volcanoes National Park, Rwanda
Tel. +27 11 257 50 00 · enquiry@wilderness.co.za
www.wilderness-safaris.com

## AMONG THE MOUNTAIN GORILLAS

Rwanda: a country whose history is eventful – and traumatic too. But also a country that aims to remember and develop, to learn and live, a country in which many people show great respect and sensitivity to its unique culture and nature. Among them those who set up Bisate Lodge, one of the most exclusive eco-lodges on the African continent. Situated on the edge of the volcanic national park in northern Rwanda, it has six villas for a maximum of twelve guests, built sustainably from local volcanic rock, granite, wood, reeds and bamboo. Inspired by the royal palace at Nyanza, the architect Garreth Kriel from Nick Plewman Architects gave the buildings spherical silhouettes and thatched roofs that refer to the shape of the surrounding hills. The interior fittings of the luxurious villas are the result of a collaboration between the South African studio Artichoke and the Rwandan designer Teta Isibo. She embellished the rooms with native craftwork, for example fabrics with traditional graphic patterns, hand-woven carpets and chandeliers of recycled glass with an emerald shimmer. The most fascinating attraction for visitors to Bisate is a trek to gorillas in the footsteps of Dian Fossey, who researched in the national park and is buried on the site. Nowhere else can you come so close to the impressive mountain gorillas, which can be observed for a brief moment under the expert direction of safari guides. The lodge also ensures that the habitat of this endangered species remains intact. Since it was opened, tens of thousands of trees have been planted as part of a reforestation program. ◆ "Gorillas in the Mist" by Dian Fossey.

DIRECTIONS *On a 67-acre site in a volcanic crater, 110 km/68 miles north-west of Kigali airport (c. 3 hours' drive)* · RATES *€€€€; all inclusive* · ROOMS *6 villas, each measuring 980 square feet with a view of the volcanoes* · FOOD *Outstanding African dishes are served in the restaurant and on the terrace* · HISTORY *Opened in June 2017* · X-FACTOR *Very exclusive and very close to nature*

# BEI DEN BERGGORILLAS

Ruanda. Ein Land mit einer wechselvollen, teilweise traumatischen Geschichte. Aber auch ein Land, das sich erinnern und entwickeln, lernen und leben will – und in dem viele Menschen viel Respekt und Sensibilität für die einzigartige Kultur und Natur zeigen. Zu ihnen zählen die Gründer der Bisate Lodge, einer der exklusivsten Ökolodges auf dem afrikanischen Kontinent. Die am Rande des Volcanoes National Park gelegenen sechs Villen der Lodge für maximal zwölf Gäste wurden nachhaltig aus lokalem Vulkanstein, Granit, Holz, Schilf sowie Bambus erbaut. Inspiriert vom Königspalast von Nyanza, verlieh Architekt Garreth Kriel von Nick Plewman Architects den Gebäuden sphärische Silhouetten und Strohdächer, welche die Form der umliegenden Hügel aufgreifen. Die Inneneinrichtung der luxuriösen Unterkünfte ist eine Zusammenarbeit des südafrikanischen Studios Artichoke und der ruandischen Designerin Teta Isibo: Sie verschönte die Räume mit einheimischem Kunsthandwerk wie Stoffen mit überlieferten Grafikmustern, handgewebten Teppichen und smaragdgrün schimmernden Kerzenleuchtern aus recyceltem Glas. Faszinierendste Attraktion für die Gäste in Bisate ist ein Gorilla-Trekking auf den Spuren von Dian Fossey, die im Nationalpark forschte und auf dem Gelände auch begraben ist. So nahe wie hier kommt man den beeindruckenden Berggorillas nirgendwo sonst. Unter fachkundiger Safarileitung kann man sie für einen kurzen Moment beobachten. Dafür, dass der Lebensraum der vom Aussterben bedrohten Spezies intakt bleibt, sorgt die Lodge ebenfalls. Seit ihrer Eröffnung wurden im Rahmen eines Aufforstungsprogrammes bereits mehrere Zehntausend Bäume gepflanzt. ◆ Buchtipp: „Briefe aus Afrika. Mein Leben mit den Gorillas" von Dian Fossey.

ANREISE *Auf einem 27 Hektar großen Areal in einem Vulkankrater gelegen, 110 km nordwestlich des Flughafens Kigali (ca. 3 Fahrtstunden) ·* PREIS *€€€€; all-inclusive ·* ZIMMER *6 Villen mit je 91 Quadratmetern, eigenem Bad und Blick auf die Vulkane ·* KÜCHE *Im Restaurant und auf der Terrasse werden ausgezeichnete afrikanische Gerichte serviert ·* GESCHICHTE *Im Juni 2017 eröffnet ·* X-FAKTOR *Sehr exklusiv und sehr naturverbunden*

# CHEZ LES GORILLES DES MONTAGNES

Le Rwanda, c'est une histoire mouvementée, en partie traumatisante. Mais c'est aussi un pays qui veut se souvenir et se développer, apprendre et vivre – et dans lequel les gens sont nombreux à montrer beaucoup de respect et de sensibilité pour cette culture et cette nature uniques. Les créateurs du Bisate Lodge, l'un des écolodges les plus nobles du continent africain, font partie de ceux-là. Situées en bordure du parc national des volcans dans le nord du Rwanda, leurs six villas qui peuvent abriter jusqu'à 12 personnes ont été construites avec des matériaux durables : pierre volcanique locale, granit, bois, roseau et bambou. S'inspirant du palais royal de Nyanza, l'architecte Garreth Kriel du cabinet d'architectes Nick Plewman a donné aux bâtiments des silhouettes sphériques et des toits de chaume qui reprennent la forme des collines environnantes. L'aménagement intérieur des logements luxueux est le fruit d'une collaboration entre le studio sud-africain Artichoke et la designer rwandaise Teta Isibo : elle a embelli les pièces avec des produits artisanaux locaux tels que des tissus aux motifs graphiques traditionnels, des tapis tissés à la main et des chandeliers en verre recyclé vert émeraude. L'attraction la plus fascinante pour les visiteurs de Bisate est une randonnée à la recherche des gorilles sur les traces de Dian Fossey, qui a fait des recherches dans le parc national et est enterrée sur le site. Nulle part ailleurs, vous ne pourrez voir de plus près les impressionnants gorilles de montagne et les observer pendant un court instant sous la direction de guides expérimentés. Le lodge veille également à ce que l'habitat des espèces en voie de disparition demeure intact. Depuis son ouverture, des dizaines de milliers d'arbres ont été plantés dans le cadre d'un programme de reboisement. ◆ À lire : « Gorilles dans la brume » de Dian Fossey.

ACCÈS *Situé sur une aire de 27 hectares sur les pentes du cratère d'un volcan, à 110 km au nord-ouest de l'aéroport de Kigali (environ 3 h de voiture) ·* PRIX *€€€€; tout compris ·* CHAMBRES *6 villas de 91 mètres carrés avec salle de bains attenante et vue sur les volcans ·* RESTAURATION *Des plats remarquables de la cuisine africaine sont servis dans le restaurant et sur a terrasse ·* HISTOIRE *Ouvert depuis juin 2017 ·* LES « PLUS » *Luxe et raffinement dans le respect de l'environnement*

# SANCTUARY GORILLA FOREST CAMP

## BWINDI IMPENETRABLE NATIONAL PARK, UGANDA

# SANCTUARY GORILLA FOREST CAMP

Bwindi Impenetrable National Park, Uganda
Tel. +254 20 248 7374 · reservations.kenya@sanctuaryretreats.com (bookings through Kenya office)
www.sanctuaryretreats.com

## GLAMPING WITH GORILLAS

This is glamping at its best, at one of Africa's most distant camps, hidden deep on a ridge high up in the marvelously named Impenetrable Forest of Bwindi. The ancient rainforest is an UNESCO World heritage site, and home to about half of the world's dwindling population of mountain gorillas. These "gentle giants" are another of our planet's endangered species. Less than a thousand remain. The atmospheric camp is close to the start point for trekking to see the remarkable animals in their natural habitat. Encounters of the managed and respectful kind are the rule. And the visits people make to their territory are sometimes reciprocated. As the gorillas roam not too far away, families of them frequently visit the camp. They appear to observe with interest those residing here in this human setting. The simple yet well-appointed tents seem to meet with their approval. The landscape around here is an impressive one. As well as dense forest, the region has volcanoes and mountain ranges, rugged valleys with dramatic waterfalls and tranquil lakes. In contrast to the imposing wildlife to be seen in this remote area, there is the opportunity for guests to interact with the local Batwa pygmies. Seeing the massive gorillas, the largest of the living primates, ranging free in the wild is on many people's "bucket list" of must-have experiences. After the guests here return from their trip, they can support their protection by donating to the International Gorilla Conservation Programme or Gorilla Fund International, set up by renowned conservationist Dian Fossey. ◆ Book to pack: "Gorillas of the Impenetrable Forest" by Carol Schaller Carmichael.

DIRECTIONS *In south-west Uganda's Bwindi Impenetrable National Park near Rwanda and Congo, 25 km/16 miles from the closest airstrip* · RATES *€€€* · ROOMS *8 luxury tents, each with en suite bathroom* · FOOD *First-class campfire dinners served under starry skies and against a panoramic jungle backdrop* · HISTORY *Established around 2004, renovated in 2018* · X-FACTOR *Apes on your doorstep: the gorilla groups often come into camp*

# GLAMPING MIT GORILLAS

Eines der entlegensten Camps in Afrika bietet Glamping in seiner schönsten Form. Es liegt auf einem Bergkamm über dem Impenetrable Forest tief im uralten „undurchdringlichen" Bwindi-Regenwald verborgen. Er ist heute UNESCO-Weltnaturerbe und beheimatet rund die Hälfte der weltweit noch existierenden Berggorillas. Die „sanften Riesen" sind akut vom Aussterben bedroht – keine 1000 von ihnen sind noch vorhanden. Das ansprechende Camp liegt nahe am Ausgangspunkt für Trekkingtouren zu den eindrucksvollen Menschenaffen in ihrem natürlichen Lebensraum. Die Begegnungen verlaufen in aller Regel behutsam und respektvoll. Und die Besuche werden erwidert: Einige Gorillafamilien machen bei Streifzügen durch die Umgebung ab und zu Abstecher ins Camp und beäugen die Menschen in ihrem eigenen Umfeld. Die dezenten, gut ausgestatteten Zelte gefallen ihnen offenbar. Rings um das Camp erstreckt sich eine einzigartige Landschaft mit dichtem Regenwald, Vulkanen und Bergketten, zerklüfteten Tälern, Wasserfällen und stillen Seen. Ein ganz großes Erlebnis neben der Tierwelt dieses entlegenen Gebiets ist eine persönliche Begegnung mit den in der Nähe ansässigen Batwa-Pygmäen. Gorillas als größte lebende Primaten in freier Wildnis beobachten zu dürfen, steht für viele auf der Liste der Dinge, die sie einmal im Leben tun möchten. Viele Camp-Gäste unterstützen den Schutz der einzigartigen Tiere mit einer Spende an das International Gorilla Conservation Program oder den Gorilla Fund International, den die bekannte Tierschützerin Dian Fossey gründete. ◆ Buchtipp: „Rote Erde, weißes Gras" von Luisa Natiwi.

**ANREISE** *Im Südwesten des Bwindi Impenetrable National Park in Uganda nahe den Grenzen zu Ruanda und zur Demokratischen Republik Kongo in 25 km Entfernung zum nächsten Flugplatz gelegen ·* **PREIS** *€€€ ·* **ZIMMER** *8 Luxuszelte mit jeweils eigenem Bad·* **KÜCHE** *Erstklassige Küche, serviert am Lagerfeuer unter dem Sternenzelt vor einem atemberaubenden Dschungelpanorama ·* **GESCHICHTE** *Um 2004 gegründet und 2018 renoviert ·* **X-FAKTOR** *Primaten hautnah erleben: Gorillagruppen besuchen regelmäßig das Camp*

# GLAMPING AVEC LES GORILLES

Voilà ce qui se fait de mieux en matière de « glamping » : un des campements les plus isolés d'Afrique, caché dans les profondeurs de la jungle, perché sur une crête de la merveilleusement nommée Forêt impénétrable de Bwindi. Cette forêt tropicale millénaire, inscrite au patrimoine mondial de l'humanité par l'UNESCO, abrite environ la moitié de la population mondiale de gorilles des montagnes, en déclin. Les « gentils géants » font partie des espèces en voie de disparition, dont il reste moins d'un millier d'individus sur terre. Le campement, chargé d'atmosphère, est proche du point de départ des randonnées à la découverte de ces animaux remarquables, dans leur habitat naturel. Les rencontres se doivent d'être encadrées et respectueuses. Et il arrive que les gorilles rendent la politesse de leur visite aux humains en entrant à leur tour sur leur territoire. Les gorilles vivent libres non loin du campement, si bien que des familles y entrent fréquemment. Il semble qu'ils observent avec intérêt les humains qui y séjournent et considèrent d'un œil plutôt approbateur leurs bungalows simples mais agréablement aménagés. Le décor alentour est impressionnant. En plus de sa forêt dense, la région est dotée de volcans et de chaînes montagneuses, de vallées accidentées qu'abreuvent des cascades spectaculaires et des lacs paisibles. Si les hôtes se trouvent au contact d'imposantes bêtes sauvages, ils auront aussi l'occasion de rencontrer la tribu locale de Pygmées, les Batwa. Voir ces majestueux gorilles, les plus grands primates vivants, évoluer librement dans la nature sauvage fait partie des expériences que bien des gens souhaiteraient vivre un jour. Une fois rentrés de leur voyage, les hôtes pourront participer à leur protection en faisant un don à l'International Gorilla Conservation Program ou à la Gorilla Fund International, fondation créée par la célèbre militante écologiste Dian Fossey. ◆ À lire : « Kintu » de Jennifer Nansubuga Makumbi.

**ACCÈS** *Au sein du parc national de Bwindi, dans le sud-ouest de l'Ouganda, près du Rwanda et de la République démocratique du Congo, à 25 km de la piste d'atterrissage la plus proche ·* **PRIX** *€€€ ·* **CHAMBRES** *8 bungalows luxueux, chacun doté d'une salle de bains ·* **RESTAURATION** *Les excellents dîners sont servis près du feu de camp, sous un ciel étincelant d'étoiles, la jungle en panorama ·* **HISTOIRE** *Inauguré vers 2004, rénové en 2018 ·* **LES « PLUS »** *Des grands singes à votre porte : les familles de gorilles viennent souvent sur le campement*

# SARARA CAMP

NAMUNYAK WILDLIFE CONSERVANCY, KENYA

# SARARA CAMP

Sessia Ltd, P.O. Box 79, Nanyuki, Kenya
Tel. +254 725 302 727 and +254 725 300 526 · info@sararacamp.com
www.sararacamp.com

## NATURAL HABITAT

By night, the sounds of Africa are not like those of other places. A whole range of sounds fills the night here and adds to its mystery. Noises you have not heard before can keep you awake, in the dark. Maybe the raspy breath of some "thing" nearby, an odd rustle and snap of twigs, or a sudden harsh cry. It is the bush orchestra tuning up – the roar of a lion, a hyena's laugh, or the shrill call of a jackal. In spite of the noise, you will nod off, and wake to early morning birdsong; and perhaps the squeal of a monkey, or the cry of the fish eagle. A spell in an African bush camp, with the sound of nature around you, and canvas walls, has an effect on all of our senses. Free from the clatter of our normal life, our hearing goes on alert. We are not used to the trumpeting of an elephant; or to the deep silence that can fall here, in such dark nights. The luxury sleeping tents at the Sarara Camp are equipped such that there is no need to go out into that night. Deep in the bush, the camp is in a vast wilderness. Yet herds still come here – of elephants, that is.

Sarara is a haven for them too. Lions are locals, along with wild dogs, zebra, giraffe and antelope. They will be at a safe distance; armed guards keep them from being too curious about you. Although difficult to spot, leopards are common; you may hear one near the camp at night. That dry cough just after you dozed off…
◆ Book to pack: "Green City in the Sun" by Barbara Wood.

DIRECTIONS *A 7-hour drive north of Nairobi, or 2 hours from Samburu; or by private air charter from Wilson Airport, Nairobi, to Namunyak airstrip ·* RATES *€€€€ ·* ROOMS *6 tents and 1 house on the main site, 8 tents in a new camp (2.5 hrs away on foot) ·* FOOD *Local, seasonal dishes, everything cooked over an open campfire – even the bread ·* HISTORY *Sarara is part of the Namunyak Wildlife Conservation Trust, working with the tribal community to protect the land and the animals ·* X-FACTOR *Bush walking and bathing in the waterfalls or pool*

# NATÜRLICH WOHNEN

Die Nacht klingt anders in Afrika. Sie ist erfüllt von einer ganzen Reihe von Geräuschen, die ihr etwas geheimnisvoll Mystisches verleihen. Fremde und neuartige Töne werden Sie in der Dunkelheit wach halten. Womöglich das heisere Atmen eines unbekannten Etwas, hier und da das Rascheln und Knacken von Zweigen oder ein plötzlicher rauer Schrei: Der Choral des afrikanischen Busches hebt an – das Brüllen eines Löwen, das Lachen einer Hyäne oder der schrille Schrei des Schakals. Trotz der Geräuschkulisse werden Sie einschlafen und früh am Morgen vom Gesang der Vögel, dem Quietschen eines Affen oder dem Schrei des Fischadlers erwachen. Ein Aufenthalt in einem afrikanischen Buschcamp berührt all unsere Sinne – vor allem wenn man zwischen Segeltuchwänden schläft und umgeben ist vom Klang der Natur. Befreit vom Alltagslärm wird unser Gehör wachsam. Weder sind wir an das Trompeten der Elefanten gewöhnt noch an die tiefe Stille, die sich in solchen dunklen Nächten über das Camp breiten kann. Die Luxuszelte sind so ausgelegt, dass Sie sie in der Nacht nicht verlassen müssen. Das Camp befindet sich tief im Innern des Busches in weiter Wildnis. Hierher kommen auch Elefantenherden, denn Sarara ist auch für sie ein sicherer Hafen. Auch Löwen, wilde Hunde, Zebras, Giraffen und Antilopen leben hier. Doch sie werden in sicherer Entfernung bleiben, während bewaffnete Wächter aufpassen, dass sie Ihnen in ihrer Neugier nicht zu nahe kommen. Auch Leoparden sind hier zu Hause. Zwar ist es schwer, sie zu entdecken, aber möglicherweise werden Sie nachts, kurz vor dem Einschlummern, ihren kratzigen Husten hören. ◆ Buchtipps: „Die weiße Massai" von Corinne Hofmann; „Rote Sonne, schwarzes Land" von Barbara Wood.

**ANREISE** *Etwa 7 Fahrtstunden nördlich von Nairobi oder 2 Fahrtstunden von Samburu; oder vom Wilson Airport, Nairobi, mit einer privaten Chartermaschine nach Namunyak fliegen* · **PREIS** *€€€€* · **ZIMMER** *6 Zelte und 1 Haus auf dem Hauptgelände, 8 Zelte in einem neuen Camp (2,5 Std. zu Fuß)* · **KÜCHE** *Lokale, saisonale Gerichte. Alles wird frisch überm Feuer zubereitet, sogar das Brot* · **GESCHICHTE** *Sarara gehört zum Namunyak Wildlife Conservation Trust und arbeitet mit der lokalen Stammesgemeinschaft zusammen, um das Land und die Tiere zu schützen* · **X-FAKTOR** *Wanderungen durch die Buschlandschaft und Baden in Wasserfällen*

# L'ÉTAT DE NATURE

Les bruits qui s'élèvent de la nuit africaine sont uniques. Toute une gamme de sons résonnent dans la nuit, ajoutant au mystère. Des bruits jusque-là inconnus peuvent vous tenir éveillé : la respiration rauque et proche d'un animal mystérieux, le bruissement et le craquement des brindilles ou un cri strident et soudain. Ce sont les instruments de l'orchestre de la brousse qui se mettent au diapason : le rugissement du lion, le rire de la hyène ou le cri perçant du chacal. Malgré tout, vous vous laisserez gagner par le sommeil, et c'est le chant matinal des oiseaux qui vous réveillera, peut-être suivi des vociférations des singes ou du cri des aigles pêcheurs. Séjourner dans un camp de brousse africain, entouré des bruits de la nature et de parois en toile, voilà qui met tous les sens en éveil. Libérée de la cacophonie de la vie quotidienne, notre ouïe est en alerte. Elle n'est pas habituée au barrissement des éléphants ou au profond silence qui règne ici une fois la nuit noire tombée. Les tentes luxueuses de Sarara Camp sont, de toute façon, si bien équipées qu'il n'est nul besoin de s'aventurer dans l'obscurité. Le camp est situé en pleine brousse, au cœur d'une vaste étendue sauvage. Pourtant, les troupeaux d'éléphants y viennent en masse. Pour eux aussi Sarara est un havre. Les animaux qui vivent ici en permanence, à savoir les lions, les chiens sauvages, les zèbres, les girafes et les antilopes, sont tenus à distance. Des gardes armés les empêchent de se montrer trop curieux à votre égard. Même s'il est difficile de les apercevoir, les léopards sont ici courants. Peut-être en entendrez-vous un rôder autour du camp, la nuit, et émettre cette toux sèche caractéristique juste au moment où vous vous assoupirez… ◆ À lire : « La Massaï blanche » de Corinne Hofmann.

**ACCÈS** *À 7 h en voiture au nord de Nairobi ou à 2 h de Samburu. Possibilité d'emprunter un avion-charter privé jusqu'à la piste d'atterrissage de Namunyak* · **PRIX** *€€€€* · **CHAMBRES** *6 tentes et une maison sur le terrain principal, 8 tentes dans un nouveau campement (2 h 30 à pied)* · **RESTAURATION** *Cuisine locale, de saison. Tout est cuit au feu de camp, même le pain* · **HISTOIRE** *Sarara fait partie du Namunyak Wildlife Conservation Trust et collabore avec la communauté tribale pour protéger l'environnement et les animaux* · **LES « PLUS »** *Promenades en brousse et baignades en piscine ou sous les chutes d'eau*

# ARIJIJU

**LEWA BORANA CONSERVANCY,
LAIKIPIA COUNTY, KENYA**

# ARIJIJU

Lewa Borana Conservancy, Timau Nandunguru Road, Nanyuki, Laikipia County, Kenya
Tel. +254 796 035 177 · arijijumanagement@arijiju.com and enquiries@arijiju.com
www.arijiju.com

## AN EXCLUSIVE REFUGE

It took ten years to complete this extraordinary estate in the Lewa Borana reservation. The search for the perfect site alone involved a great deal of research: the owners, both wealthy and discreet, whose roots are in Nigeria and Norway, took a lot of time to study the play of wind, sun and shadows, and to find the most beautiful view of sunrise, sunset and Mount Kenya. They also hired architects of international renown: Alex Michaelis from London and Nick Plewman from Johannesburg, who took inspiration when designing the house from the work of Kenyan artisans, Ethiopian rock churches and the monastery of Le Thoronet in the south of France. With its grass-covered flat roof, walls of rough Meru stone and strong wooden gates, Arijiju nestles into the hill after which it is named, as if it belongs there. Its interior fittings bear the signature of Maira Koutsoudakis, who has already designed such precious jewels as North Island in the Seychelles. In a style that is simultaneously highly sensual, reticent but luxurious, she has combined furniture hand-made locally with antiques and accessories from Africa and Europe – keeping to earthy colors, presented in the right light by opulent crystal chandeliers. Actually conceived as a private residence, Arijiju is rented to guests on request – for exclusive use – with five double bedrooms, a library and cinema, pool and spa. The service includes a team of fourteen: cooks, butlers and rangers, who give expert tours through the surrounding reservation, a habitat of the legendary Big Five. ◆ Book to pack: "Rafiki" by Meja Mwangi.

**DIRECTIONS** *About 230 km/140 miles north of Nairobi (4 hours' drive). The nearest airstrips for light aircraft are Lewa (90 minutes) and Borana (15 minutes). Arijiju also has its own helicopter pad ·* **ROOMS** *5 suites. An extra is the Constellation Suite on the roof terrace, for a night beneath the stars ·* **RATES** *€€€€; the estate is available for exclusive hire only ·* **FOOD** *Healthy, fine and fresh down-to-earth cooking – with many ingredients from Arijiju's own organic garden ·* **HISTORY** *Opened in November 2016 ·* **X-FACTOR** *The owners are actively engaged in preserving and developing the reservation*

# EIN EXKLUSIVES REFUGIUM

Es dauerte zehn Jahre, bis dieses außergewöhnliche Anwesen im Naturschutzgebiet von Lewa Borana fertiggestellt war. Allein die Suche nach dem perfekten Bauplatz war eine Wissenschaft für sich: Die ebenso wohlhabenden wie diskreten Eigentümer, deren Wurzeln in Nigeria und Norwegen liegen, nahmen sich viel Zeit, um das Spiel von Wind, Sonne und Schatten zu studieren und die schönste Sicht auf Sonnenaufgang, Sonnenuntergang sowie den Mount Kenya zu finden. Zudem engagierten sie Architekten von internationalem Ruf: Alex Michaelis aus London und Nick Plewman aus Johannesburg ließen sich beim Entwurf des Hauses von kenianischer Handwerkskunst, äthiopischen Felsenkirchen und dem südfranzösischen Kloster Le Thoronet inspirieren. Mit seinem grasbewachsenen Flachdach, Mauern aus grob behauenem Meru-Stein und mächtigen Holzportalen schmiegt sich Arijiju wie selbstverständlich an den Hügel, nach dem die Lodge benannt ist. Ihre Inneneinrichtung trägt die Handschrift von Maira Koutsoudakis, die bereits so wertvolle Juwelen wie North Island auf den Seychellen designt hat. Sehr sinnlich, zurückhaltend und luxuriös zugleich kombinierte sie vor Ort handgefertigte Möbel mit Antiquitäten und Accessoires aus Afrika und Europa – immer in Erdtönen gehalten und von opulenten Kristalllüstern ins rechte Licht gesetzt. Eigentlich als private Residenz konzipiert, wird Arijiju auf Anfrage aber auch an Gäste vermietet – exklusiv mit fünf Doppelzimmern, Bibliothek, Kino, Pool und Spa. Ebenfalls zum Service gehört ein 14-köpfiges Team von Köchen, Butlern und Rangern, die fachkundig durchs umliegende Reservat führen, in dem die „Big Five" (Löwe, Elefant, Büffel, Leopard und Nashorn) leben. ◆ Buchtipp: „Rafiki" von Meja Mwangi.

**ANREISE** *Rund 230 km nördlich von Nairobi gelegen (4 Fahrtstunden). Nächstliegende Landeplätze für Kleinflugzeuge sind Lewa (90 Min.) sowie Borana (15 Min.). Arijiju besitzt außerdem einen eigenen Helikopterlandeplatz ·* **ZIMMER** *5 Suiten, zudem als Extra die Constellation Suite auf der Dachterrasse für eine Nacht unter freiem Himmel ·* **PREIS** *€€€€; das Anwesen kann nur exklusiv gemietet werden ·* **KÜCHE** *Gesunde, feine und frische Hausmannskost – der eigene Biogarten liefert viele Zutaten ·* **GESCHICHTE** *Im November 2016 eröffnet ·* **X-FAKTOR** *Die Besitzer setzen sich aktiv für Schutz und Entwicklung des Reservats ein*

# UN REFUGE UNIQUE

Il a fallu dix ans pour réaliser cette propriété exceptionnelle dans le site protégé de Lewa Borana. La recherche du lieu de construction idéal a été une science en soi : les propriétaires, aussi riches que discrets, dont les racines se trouvent au Nigeria et en Norvège, ont pris le temps d'étudier le jeu du vent, du soleil et de l'ombre et de trouver les plus belles vues du lever et du coucher du soleil et du Mont Kenya. Ils ont également engagé des architectes de renommée internationale : Alex Michaelis de Londres et Nick Plewman de Johannesburg se sont inspirés de l'artisanat kenyan, des églises rupestres éthiopiennes et du monastère du Thoronet dans le sud de la France. Avec son toit plat végétalisé, ses murs de pierre brute de Méru et ses imposants portails en bois, Arijiju se blottit tout naturellement contre la colline qui lui a donné son nom. L'aménagement intérieur porte la griffe de Maira Koutsoudakis, qui a déjà conçu des petits joyaux comme le North Island aux Seychelles. Très sensuel, sobre et luxueux à la fois, il associe des meubles fabriqués par des artisans locaux avec des antiquités et des accessoires d'Afrique et d'Europe, toujours dans des tons de terre et mis en valeur par des lustres en cristal opulents. Conçu à l'origine comme une résidence privée, Arijiju peut être loué à la demande – exclusivement, avec cinq chambres doubles, bibliothèque et cinéma, piscine et spa. Le service est assuré par une équipe de 14 personnes, chefs cuisiniers, majordomes et rangers, qui vous guideront à travers la réserve environnante où vivent les légendaires « Big Five » – les cinq plus grands mammifères africains. ◆ À lire : « Kariuki » de Meja Mwangi.

**ACCÈS** *Situé à 230 km au nord de Nairobi (4 h de voiture). Les aires d'atterrissage les plus proches pour les petits avions se trouvent à Lewa (90 min) et Borana (15 min). Arijiju possède en outre une aire d'atterrissage privée pour les hélicoptères ·* **CHAMBRES** *5 suites. En extra la Constellation Suite sur le toit-terrasse pour passer une nuit à la belle étoile ·* **PRIX** *€€€€; la propriété ne peut être louée qu'à usage exclusif ·* **RESTAURATION** *Des plats légers, frais et raffinés – le jardin bio livre de nombreux produits ·* **HISTOIRE** *Ouvert en novembre 2016 ·* **LES « PLUS »** *Les propriétaires participent activement à la protection et au développement de la réserve naturelle*

# DODO'S TOWER

### LAKE NAIVASHA, KENYA

# DODO'S TOWER

Lake Naivasha, Nairobi, Kenya
Tel. +254 733 333 014 · info@hippopointkenya.com
www.hippopointkenya.com

## TOWERING ASPIRATIONS

Once upon a time, when I was a child, the tale of a girl kept in a tower was one of my favorites. "Rapunzel, Rapunzel, let down your golden hair"; the words the witch, and the prince, called to make her send her lengthy locks down to the ground was a line I loved. However, the tower in the Brothers Grimm story was as bleak as the fable. It had neither door nor staircase, and only one very high window. This is much more like a fairy-tale tower, and it's a real one. Dodo's Tower is a whimsical formation on the shores of an enchanting lake; it is one of the most fanciful places to stay in all of Africa. Just its tip can be seen above a forest of acacia trees, yet the rest of it blends quite naturally into the background. At some times of the morning and night, it can trick the eye, morphing more into a tree trunk than a building. A closer look reveals that a playful yet sure hand, one that loves luxury as much as fantasy, has shaped it. The stylish pagoda is the happy ending to a dream that others can share. It seems to cast a benign spell over all who come here. Having a wooden spire in the middle of the landscape does not seem to phase the creatures that share this setting. Hippos and giraffes, or pelicans and flamingos seldom play a part in fables; yet they can be seen far below from the verandas of this imaginative place. ◆ Books to pack: Several, so that you need not come down…: "The Lord of the Rings: The Two Towers" by J. R. R. Tolkien; "The Seven Story Tower" by Curtiss Hoffman, "The Ebony Tower" by John Fowles; "Child of Happy Valley" by Juanita Carberry.

**DIRECTIONS** *A 20-minute charter flight from Nairobi to Naivasha airstrip and then a 10-minute drive to the estate. By road, the estate is a 2-hour drive north-west from Nairobi ·* **RATES** *€€€€ ·* **ROOMS** *5, on four floors, with a meditation room at the very top ·* **FOOD** *International-inspired dishes with ingredients from the on-site organic vegetable garden ·* **HISTORY** *Built in the early 1990s on the same estate as Hippo Point ·* **X-FACTOR** *The chance to be in a fairy tale of your own*

# EIN MÄRCHENTURM

Es war einmal ein Märchen … Als ich ein Kind war, gehörte die Geschichte von dem Mädchen, das in einem Turm gefangen gehalten wurde, zu meinen Lieblingserzählungen. „Rapunzel, Rapunzel, lass dein goldenes Haar herunter." Ich liebte diese Stelle, wenn die Hexe und der Prinz jene Worte riefen, damit das Mädchen seine langen Locken herunterließ. Trotzdem – der Turm in der Geschichte der Gebrüder Grimm ist so düster wie die Erzählung selbst. Er hatte weder eine Tür noch eine Treppe und nur ein einziges, sehr hoch gelegenes Fenster. Der Turm, von dem hier die Rede ist, sieht aus wie ein Märchenturm, doch er ist echt! Dodo's Tower ist ein skurriles Gebäude am Ufer eines bezaubernden Sees, einem der fantastischsten Orte in Afrika. Man kann nur seine Spitze aus einem Akazienwald herausragen sehen; der übrige Teil fügt sich ganz natürlich in die Umgebung ein. Manchmal, im frühen Morgen- oder Abendlicht, ähnelt der Turm, wie durch eine optische Täuschung, eher einem alten Baumstamm als einem Gebäude. Bei genauerem Hinsehen wird jedoch deutlich, dass dies ein spielerisches, aber dennoch exakt geplantes Werk ist, erbaut von jemandem, der Luxus und Fantasie gleichermaßen liebt. Die stilvolle Pagode ist wie ein wahr gewordener Traum und scheint jeden mit einer Art gutem Zauber zu belegen. Der hölzerne Turm inmitten der Landschaft stört die dort lebenden Tiere offenbar keineswegs. Nilpferde und Giraffen, Pelikane und Flamingos kommen in Märchen eher selten vor. Doch von seiner Veranda aus kann man sie weit unter sich sehen. ◆ Buchtipps: Gleich mehrere, damit Sie nicht vom Turm herunterkommen müssen … : „Der Herr der Ringe. Die zwei Türme" von J. R. R. Tolkien; „Letzte Tage in Kenia. Meine Kindheit in Afrika" von Juanita Carberry; „Sehnsucht nach Kenia. Ein afrikanisches Reisetagebuch" von Hannelore Kornherr.

**ANREISE** *Mit einer privaten Chartermaschine etwa 20 Min. von Nairobi nach Naivasha, anschließend 10-minütige Fahrt zum Anwesen. Mit dem Wagen 2 Fahrtstunden nordwestlich von Nairobi ·* **PREIS** *€€€€ ·* **ZIMMER** *5 Zimmer auf vier Stockwerken, im obersten ein Meditationsraum ·* **KÜCHE** *International inspirierte Gerichte mit Zutaten aus dem eigenen Biogarten ·* **GESCHICHTE** *In den frühen 1990er-Jahren erbaut. Befindet sich auf demselben Grundstück wie das Hippo Point ·* **X-FAKTOR** *Die Chance, in einem Märchen zu leben*

# AU-DESSUS DES GIRAFES

Lorsque j'étais enfant, l'un de mes contes favoris était celui narrant l'histoire d'une jeune fille enfermée dans une tour. « Rapunzel, Rapunzel, détache tes cheveux blonds. » J'adorais ces mots que la sorcière et le prince adressaient à la jeune fille pour la convaincre de laisser tomber sa chevelure jusqu'au sol. Pourtant, la tour du conte des frères Grimm, sans porte ni escalier et dotée d'une unique et haute fenêtre, était aussi lugubre que la fable elle-même. Dodo's Tower est plus conforme à l'image habituelle d'une tour de conte de fées, et elle est bien réelle. Construction insolite installée sur les rives d'un lac enchanteur, il s'agit de l'un des hôtels les plus originaux de toute l'Afrique. Seul son sommet dépasse d'une forêt d'acacias, le reste de son architecture se fondant naturellement dans le paysage. À certaines heures du matin et du soir, vos yeux peuvent vous jouer des tours et donner à l'édifice l'apparence d'un tronc d'arbre. Mais en y regardant de plus près, on s'aperçoit qu'il a été façonné par une main espiègle mais habile, amatrice de luxe tout autant que de fantaisie. L'élégante pagode est l'heureux dénouement d'un rêve que les visiteurs sont invités à partager, et tous sont immédiatement envoûtés. La présence de cette flèche de bois au milieu du paysage ne semble pas troubler les créatures qui partagent le territoire. Les fables ne mettent jamais en scène les hippopotames, les girafes, les pélicans ou les flamants roses. Ici, installés dans la véranda de ce lieu plein d'imagination, vous pourrez toutefois les voir évoluer loin en contrebas. ◆ À lire : plusieurs suggestions, pour ne pas avoir à redescendre… : « Le Seigneur des Anneaux. Les Deux Tours » de J. R. R. Tolkien ; « La tour d'Ébène » de John Fowles ; « Valjoie » de Nathaniel Hawthorne.

**ACCÈS** *En avion, vol Nairobi-Naivasha d'une durée de 20 min, puis 10 min en voiture. Au nord-ouest de Nairobi, à 2 h en voiture ·* **PRIX** *€€€€ ·* **CHAMBRES** *5, réparties sur quatre étages, avec salle de méditation au dernier ·* **RESTAURATION** *Plats d'inspiration internationale cuisinés avec les ingrédients du jardin bio ·* **HISTOIRE** *Construite au début des années 1990 sur la même propriété que le Hippo Point ·* **LES « PLUS »** *Un véritable conte de fées*

# HIPPO POINT

**LAKE NAIVASHA, KENYA**

# HIPPO POINT

Lake Naivasha, Naivasha, Kenya
Tel. +254 733 993 713 · office@hippopointkenya.com
www.hippopointkenya.com

## VESTIGES OF ENGLAND

There are no fairies at the bottom of this English garden. Instead, the real reverse of those fantasy and lighter-than-air creatures live here. Hundreds of "river horses", as the Greeks once called them, or hippopotami, as we know them now, are just outside the fence. They like to eat the flowers, so they must be kept out. Hippo Point is set in a garden of fragrant roses and verdant lawns; a mock-Tudor manor in classic grounds leading down to a pretty lake. So far, it is a scene typical in an English landscape, but it is in the heart of Kenya's Great Rift Valley. That makes the livestock to be seen here even more of a contrast to the house. The lovely old home was built in the 1930s in the romantic style popular in England then. Its original owners had been transplanted to "deepest darkest Africa"; to them, this house and garden was a token of their native land thousands of miles away. Years later it was found in ruins, but reinvented as a fine guesthouse. Under its gabled roof, the elegant rooms are furnished with antiques, more memories of a distant Europe. Inside, it could still be a corner of England. Once outside, the difference is of course clear. This is a sanctuary; giraffe, hippo, antelope, zebra, and leopards, and hundreds of different sorts of birds live here. The sounds, and scents, of Africa and England are worlds apart. ◆ Books to pack: "White Mischief" by James Fox; "The Hippopotamus" by Stephen Fry.

DIRECTIONS *By air, a 20-minute charter from Nairobi to Naivasha airstrip, and then a 10-minute drive to the estate. By road, a 2-hour drive north-west from Nairobi* · RATES €€€€ · ROOMS *8 rooms for up to 15 people* · FOOD *Mediterranean-inspired dishes with fresh ingredients from the on-site organic garden* · HISTORY *Built in the 1930s, and much later Dodo's Tower, the folly, was built on the same property by the present owners* · X-FACTOR *Seeming to have a foot in two countries*

# ENGLISCHE REMINISZENZEN

Elfen, die ja angeblich in jedem echten englischen Garten zu finden sind, gibt es hier zwar keine, dafür aber das genaue Gegenteil dieser zarten Fantasiegestalten, die leichter sind als Luft. Direkt hinter dem Zaun leben Hunderte von Flusspferden oder Hippopotami, wie sie schon die alten Griechen nannten. Der Zaun soll sie davon abhalten, die Blumen zu fressen. Das Hippo Point liegt inmitten eines duftenden grünen Rosengartens. Es wurde einem Tudorgut nachempfunden, und seine klassische Parkanlage führt zu einem kleinen See hinab. Bis hierher klingt dies alles nach einem typisch englischen Schauplatz, doch er liegt im Herzen von Kenias Great Rift Valley. Die Tiere, die man hier beobachten kann, bilden dadurch einen umso stärkeren Kontrast zu dem Haus. Das bezaubernde alte Gebäude wurde in den 1930er-Jahren erbaut – gemäß dem romantischen Stil, der zu jener Zeit in England so beliebt war. Seine ursprünglichen Besitzer waren gezwungen gewesen, in das „tiefste, schwärzeste Afrika" zu ziehen, deshalb stellten für sie dieses Haus und der Garten eine Art Verbindungsglied dar zu ihrer Tausende von Kilometern entfernten Heimat. Jahre später, das Haus war mittlerweile eine Ruine, entdeckte man es neu und baute es zu einem Hotel um. Unter seinem Giebeldach befinden

sich elegante Räume, die – ausgestattet mit Antiquitäten – Erinnerungen an das ferne Europa wachrufen. Die Innenräume könnten tatsächlich in irgendeinem Winkel Englands liegen. Doch sobald man aus dem Gebäude heraustritt, wird der Unterschied selbstverständlich sofort offensichtlich: Dies ist ein unberührtes Wildreservat, in welchem Giraffen, Flusspferde, Antilopen, Zebras, Leoparden sowie Hunderte verschiedener Vogelarten leben. Zwischen den Geräuschen und Gerüchen Afrikas und Englands liegen wahrhaftig Welten. ◆ Buchtipps: „Weißes Verhängnis" von James Fox; „Das Nilpferd" von Stephen Fry.

ANREISE *Ein etwa 20-minütiger Flug mit einer privaten Chartermaschine von Nairobi nach Naivasha. Von dort aus 10-minütige Fahrt zum Anwesen. Mit dem Wagen 2 Fahrtstunden nordwestlich von Nairobi ·* PREIS *€€€€ ·* ZIMMER *8 Zimmer für bis zu 15 Gäste ·* KÜCHE *Mediterran inspirierte Küche mit frischen Zutaten aus dem eigenen Biogarten ·* GESCHICHTE *Erbaut in den 1930er-Jahren; auf demselben Grundstück errichteten die heutigen Besitzer viel später Dodo's Tower ·* X-FAKTOR *Zwei Kulturen an einem Ort*

# VESTIGES D'ANGLETERRE

Au fond de ce jardin anglais, tout droit sorties d'un conte de fées, évoluent des créatures aux antipodes de ces êtres fantastiques et gracieux. Des centaines d'hippopotames, ou « chevaux de rivière » comme les appelaient les Grecs, vivent en effet juste de l'autre côté de la clôture. Étant donné leur goût prononcé pour les fleurs, l'entrée du site leur est interdite. Le Hippo Point, imitation d'un manoir Tudor, est installé sur un domaine d'agencement classique descendant jusqu'à un lac charmant, au milieu d'un jardin de roses odorantes et de pelouses verdoyantes. Ce cadre, qui s'apparente à un paysage anglais typique, se trouve en réalité au cœur de la grande vallée du Rift, au Kenya, d'où le fort contraste entre la propriété et la faune alentour. Cette jolie vieille demeure fut construite dans les années 1930 dans le style romantique alors en vogue en Angleterre. Pour ses premiers propriétaires, transplantés « au plus profond de l'Afrique noire », la maison et son jardin symbolisaient leur pays natal, à des milliers de kilomètres de là. Des années plus tard, la bâtisse, alors en ruine, fut restaurée et retrouva une nouvelle vie en tant que pension de famille raffinée.

Protégées par un toit à double pente, les chambres élégantes sont meublées d'antiquités, autres souvenirs d'une Europe lointaine. Encore aujourd'hui, une fois à l'intérieur, on pourrait se croire en Angleterre. Mais dès que l'on met le pied dehors, la différence saute aux yeux : des girafes, des hippopotames, des antilopes, des zèbres, des léopards et des centaines d'espèces d'oiseaux vivent dans cette réserve naturelle. Et les sons et les parfums de l'Afrique n'ont rien à voir avec ceux de l'Angleterre. ◆ À lire : « Je rêvais de l'Afrique » de Kuki Gallmann ; « L'hippopotame » de Stephen Fry.

ACCÈS *Trajet de 20 min en avion de Nairobi jusqu'à la piste d'atterrissage de Naivasha, puis 10 min en voiture jusqu'à la propriété. À 2 h au nord-ouest de Nairobi en voiture ·* PRIX *€€€€ ·* CHAMBRES *8 chambres pouvant accueillir jusqu'à 15 personnes ·* RESTAURATION *Plats d'inspiration méditerranéenne cuisinés avec les produits frais du jardin bio ·* HISTOIRE *Date des années 1930. Les propriétaires actuels ont fait construire Dodo's Tower bien plus tard ·* LES « PLUS » *Impression d'être dans deux pays différents à la fois*

# THE GIRAFFE MANOR

## NEAR NAIROBI, KENYA

# THE GIRAFFE MANOR

P.O. Box 15565, Langata, 00503 Nairobi, Kenya
Tel. +254 725 675 830 and +254 731 914 732 · info@thesafaricollection.com
www.thesafaricollection.com

## VISITS FROM GIRAFFES

This elegant house was here before the giraffes; but luckily, it was constructed as a two-storey building, so that now the statuesque creatures can be fed at a height that best suits them. There are some benefits in being so tall. Gazing through the upper windows as they stroll by is a usual bent for them, though it might be surprising for guests. The Giraffe Manor is home to several of these bizarre yet beautiful animals. The ones that live here in the acres of forest are rare Rothschild giraffes, descendants of what were once an endangered species. In the 1970s, the former house owners set up the African Fund for Endangered Wildlife: a name that was soon and aptly shortened to AFEW. They transferred five baby giraffes to their property, with the result that they are on record as being the only people to have successfully brought up wild giraffes. Those are now grown-up with babies of their own. There is a human story here too. One of the bedrooms is furnished with pieces that Karen Blixen, author of "Out of Africa", gave to the owners when she left Kenya. And upstairs, in the hall, are the bookcases that the love of her life, Denys Finch Hatton, made for her. The world's tallest animal does not have the sole advantage of height here; the snow-capped peak of Kilimanjaro, the highest mountain in Africa, can be seen in the distance. "African legend insists that man arrived on earth by sliding down the giraffe's neck from Heaven…" Betty Leslie-Melville, co-founder with Jock Leslie-Melville of AFEW ◆ Book to pack: "Zarafa" by Michael Allin.

DIRECTIONS *20 km/12 miles south-west of Nairobi; 20 minutes from the airport* · RATES *€€€€* · ROOMS *12 bedrooms with bathrooms* · FOOD *The chef focuses on providing for the guests, not the giraffes* · HISTORY *Built in 1932* · X-FACTOR *You rarely get so close to giraffes as here!*

# GIRAFFEN ZU BESUCH

Dieses elegante Haus stand bereits hier, bevor die Giraffen da waren; doch glücklicherweise wurde es zweistöckig konstruiert, sodass die stattlich hohen Tiere aus optimaler Höhe gefüttert werden können. So groß zu sein, hat einige Vorteile. Und während es für die Hotelgäste durchaus überraschend sein mag, ist es für die Giraffen ganz normal, dass sie einen Blick durch die oberen Fenster werfen, wenn sie draußen vorbeistolzieren. Giraffe Manor beheimatet gleich mehrere dieser bizarren und doch gleichzeitig so schönen Kreaturen. Die Tiere, die in diesem mehrere Hektar großen Waldgebiet leben, gehören zur Spezies der seltenen Rothschild-Giraffe und sind somit Nachkommen einer einst vom Aussterben bedrohten Art. In den 1970er-Jahren riefen die damaligen Besitzer des Hauses den Afrikanischen Fond Existenzbedrohter Wildtierarten ins Leben („African Fund for Endangered Wildlife"), ein Name, der bald darauf kurz und prägnant zu AFEW abgekürzt wurde. Sie siedelten fünf Babygiraffen auf ihrem Grundstück an und sind seither bekannt dafür, die einzigen Menschen zu sein, die es jemals geschafft haben, wilde Giraffen großzuziehen. Hier gibt es jedoch auch eine Geschichte von Menschen zu erzählen.

Eines der Schlafzimmer wurde mit Möbeln ausgestattet, die Tania Blixen, die Autorin von „Jenseits von Afrika", den Besitzern schenkte, als sie Kenia verließ. Und oben, in der Halle, stehen die Bücherregale, die Denys Finch Hatton, die Liebe ihres Lebens, für sie gezimmert hatte. Das größte Tier der Welt ist nicht das Einzige, was hier einen Anspruch auf die Bezeichnung groß oder hoch erheben kann: In der Ferne kann man die schneebedeckte Kuppe des höchsten Berges in Afrika erkennen – die Spitze des Kilimandscharo. „Die afrikanische Welterschaffungslegende besagt, dass der Mensch vom Himmel auf die Erde kam, indem er einen Giraffenhals hinabrutschte …" Betty Leslie-Melville, Mitbegründerin von AFEW gemeinsam mit Jock Leslie-Melville ◆ Buchtipp: „Zarafa" von Michael Allin.

ANREISE *20 km südwestlich von Nairobi entfernt; 20 Min. vom Flughafen* · PREIS *€€€€* · ZIMMER *12 Zimmer mit Bad* · KÜCHE *Der Koch konzentriert sich darauf, die Gäste zu verwöhnen, nicht die Giraffen* · GESCHICHTE *Erbaut im Jahre 1932* · X-FAKTOR *So nahe wie hier kommt man Giraffen selten!*

# VISITES AMICALES DES GIRAFES

Cet élégant édifice existait avant l'arrivée des girafes. Fort heureusement, l'architecte avait prévu deux étages, et l'on peut aujourd'hui nourrir ces créatures sculpturales depuis une hauteur appropriée. Il y a des avantages à être grand. Les girafes sont curieuses et ont tendance à venir regarder longuement au travers des fenêtres les plus hautes lors de leurs déambulations, même si cela peut prendre au dépourvu les clients de l'hôtel. Giraffe Manor abrite plusieurs de ces étranges et magnifiques animaux. Les girafes qui vivent ici, dans l'immense forêt, sont des animaux rares, les girafes Rothschild, descendantes d'une espèce autrefois en voie d'extinction. Dans les années 1970, les anciens propriétaires fondèrent l'African Fund for Endangered Wildlife (Fonds africain pour les espèces menacées), rapidement abrégé en AFEW, et transférèrent cinq girafons dans leur propriété. C'est la seule expérience réussie au monde d'un élevage de girafes sauvages, aujourd'hui adultes et à leur tour mamans. L'homme a aussi apporté sa pierre à l'histoire de ce lieu. L'une des chambres est en effet garnie d'objets donnés par Karen Blixen, l'auteur de « La ferme africaine » (« Out of Africa ») avant son départ du Kenya. En outre, dans le hall du premier étage se trouvent les bibliothèques fabriquées pour elle par l'amour de sa vie, Denys Finch Hatton. L'animal le plus grand du monde n'a pas le monopole de la hauteur : vous apercevrez à l'horizon les sommets enneigés du Kilimandjaro, la montagne la plus haute d'Afrique. « La légende africaine veut que l'Homme soit arrivé du paradis sur la terre en glissant le long du cou d'une girafe… » Betty Leslie-Melville, cofondatrice de l'AFEW avec Jock Leslie-Melville ◆ À lire : « La girafe de Charles X » de Michael Allin.

ACCÈS *À 20 km au sud-ouest de Nairobi et à 20 min de l'aéroport* · PRIX *€€€€* · CHAMBRES *12 chambres avec salle de bains* · RESTAURATION *Le chef cuisinier se consacre aux clients et non aux girafes !* · HISTOIRE *Construit en 1932* · LES « PLUS » *Vous nourrirez les girafes depuis votre chambre à l'étage ou depuis la terre ferme, il est rare de les voir de si près*

# COTTAR'S 1920s SAFARI CAMP

## MASAI MARA NATIONAL RESERVE, KENYA

# COTTAR'S 1920s SAFARI CAMP

Masai Mara National Reserve, Kenya
Tel. +254 770 564 911 · info@cottarsafaris.com
www.cottars.com/1920s-camp

## FAR FROM THE MADDING CROWD

This romantic haven is sited in the Olderkesi area, very close to the Masai Mara, the famous game reserve some say is the seventh natural wonder of the world. It is the only safari camp in literally thousands of acres. Privacy is assured, at least from other people, although there is a long-established passageway for migrating wildlife in the vicinity. Thousands of zebra, gazelles and wildebeest travel to and from the Serengeti every year. Guests on game viewing drives will likely spot all or some of the famous "Big Five"– the lion, elephant, buffalo, leopard and rhinoceros – as well as the very tall ones – giraffes. Cottar's is a classic retreat with the look of a glamorous movie set portraying the way it used to be, on luxury safari in the past. This is how it is at present, a stylishness polished and enhanced over many years by the family who started it and run it still. The grandly furnished tents, some with fireplaces, are more rooms that just happen to have walls made of canvas. Its vintage charm is of course complemented with contemporary luxuries. Between game drives, guests can swim in the pool or bask in the sun. Some may choose to have an authentic old style safari bath, outdoors in a canvas tub, in full view of the great savanna that spreads out into the distance. The Masai people are the ancestral inhabitants of the area, and own the land the camp is on. There is a close and supportive relationship. Guests are offered authentic cultural visits and a unique opportunity to take part in a Masai warrior school. ◆ Book to pack: "The Flame Trees of Thika" by Elspeth Huxley.

DIRECTIONS *Cottar's private airstrip is a 10-minutes drive from the camp; Keekorak airstrip is a 1.5-hour drive to the camp ·* RATES €€€€ · ROOMS *4 two-person tents, 4 tents for families, and 1 honeymoon tent; VIPs and large families can rent the private bush house, which has 5 en suite bedrooms ·* FOOD *International high-end bush cuisine ·* HISTORY *The camp opened in the mid-1990s; Cottar's Safari Service began in 1919 ·* X-FACTOR *The feeling of being on a glamorous film set, in the golden era of safari*

## FERNAB VOM TRUBEL DER WELT

Das romantische Refugium liegt im Gebiet von Olderkesi nah am berühmten Naturschutzgebiet Masai Mara, das viele für das siebte Weltwunder halten. Es ist das einzige Safari-Camp im Umkreis von über 1500 Hektar. Ihre Privatsphäre ist perfekt geschützt – zumindest vor Ihren Artgenossen, denn Tausende Zebras, Gazellen und Gnus wandern jedes Jahr ganz in der Nähe durch einen uralten Korridor zur Serengeti und zurück. Bei den Fotosafaris sieht man in der Regel mehrere, oft auch alle der berühmten „Big Five" (Löwe, Elefant, Büffel, Leopard und Nashorn) und Giraffen. Im Cottar's fühlt man sich in das glamouröse Set für einen Film über die klassischen Luxussafaris der Goldenen Zwanziger versetzt. Der bis heute makellose Chic wird seit vielen Jahren von der Familie gepflegt, die das Camp gründete und auch jetzt noch leitet. Die grandios ausgestatteten Zelte, einige davon mit offenem Kamin, sind eigentlich Salons mit Wänden aus Zeltbahnen. Der Charme der Zwanziger wird natürlich noch versüßt durch zeitgemäßen Luxus. Zwischen zwei Fotosafaris können die Gäste im Pool schwimmen oder sich in der Sonne aalen. Wer mag, kann im echten Safaristil mit Savannenblick bis zum Horizont in der Segeltuchwanne im Freien ein zünftiges Bad nehmen oder duschen. Zu den Massai, denen seit Menschengedenken das ganze Gebiet gehört und damit auch das Grundstück des Camps, besteht eine enge, freundschaftliche Beziehung. Die Camp-Gäste sind eingeladen, die authentische Kultur dieses Volkes kennenzulernen und sogar die Ausbildung der Massai-Krieger mitzuerleben. ♦ Buchtipp: „Die Flammenbäume von Thika" von Elspeth Huxley.

ANREISE *Cottar's Start- und Landebahn liegt 10 Min., der Flugplatz Keekorak rund 1,5 Std. vom Camp entfernt* · PREIS €€€€ · ZIMMER *4 Zweipersonenzelte, 4 Familienzelte, 1 Zelt für frisch Verheiratete. VIPs und Großfamilien können die private Buschvilla mieten, die 5 Schlafzimmer mit jeweils eigenem Bad besitzt* · KÜCHE *Internationale gehobene Buschküche* · GESCHICHTE *Das Camp wurde Mitte der 1990er-Jahre eröffnet. Cottar's Safari Service gibt es seit 1919* · X-FAKTOR *Das Gefühl, man sei mitten in einem atemberaubenden Filmset in der Glanzzeit der Safaris*

## LOIN DE LA FOULE DÉCHAÎNÉE

Ce havre romantique est situé dans la région d'Olderkesi, tout près du Massaï Mara, la célèbre réserve dont certains disent qu'elle est la septième merveille naturelle du monde. Ce campement de safari est bel et bien le seul à des milliers d'hectares à la ronde. Intimité assurée, en tout cas pour ce qui est d'autres humains, car les animaux en migration, eux, passent là depuis des générations. Des milliers de zèbres, de gazelles et d'autres animaux sauvages se déplacent vers et depuis le Serengeti chaque année. Les hôtes amateurs de safaris-photos repéreront sûrement quelques-uns des « Cinq Grands » de la savane – le lion, l'éléphant, le buffle, le léopard et le rhinocéros – ainsi que les très grandes girafes. Cottar's est un refuge classique. Il évoque le décor chic d'un film qui montrerait le safari de luxe tel qu'il était pratiqué dans le passé, un lieu figé dans le temps grâce à une finesse stylistique que la famille qui a lancé l'affaire et la tient toujours a lustrée et accentuée au fil du temps. Les tentes meublées avec opulence, certaines dotées d'une cheminée, ressemblent davantage à des chambres dont les cloisons se trouvent être en toile. Leur charme vintage est bien sûr complété par des produits de luxe plus contemporains. Entre deux safaris-photos, les hôtes nageront dans la piscine ou se prélasseront au soleil. Certains choisiront de prendre un vrai bain de brousse à l'ancienne, en extérieur dans une baignoire en toile, d'autres opteront pour la douche face à la savane qui s'étend à perte de vue. Les Massaï sont les premiers habitants de la région et possèdent la terre sur laquelle se trouve le campement. L'interaction et le soutien mutuel règnent. Les hôtes profitent de visites culturelles authentiques et d'une chance unique de suivre les enseignements de l'école des guerriers Massaï. ♦ À lire : « Les pionniers du Kenya » d'Elspeth Huxley.

ACCÈS *La piste d'atterrissage privée du Cottar's est à 10 min du campement en voiture ; l'aérodrome de Keekorak est à 1 h 30 de route* · PRIX €€€€ · CHAMBRES *4 tentes doubles, 4 tentes familiales et une spéciale lune de miel ; les personnalités et grandes familles peuvent louer la villa du bush privée qui abrite 5 chambres pourvues chacune d'une salle de bains* · RESTAURATION *Cuisine internationale de brousse haut de gamme* · HISTOIRE *Le campement a ouvert au milieu des années 1990, mais le service Safari du Cottar's existe depuis 1919* · LES « PLUS » *La sensation d'être dans un somptueux décor de cinéma durant l'âge d'or du safari*

# PEPONI HOTEL

**LAMU, KENYA**

# PEPONI HOTEL

Lamu, Kenya
Tel. +254 722 203 082 and +254 703 790 411 · reservations@peponihotel.com
www.peponi-lamu.com

## TRADING PLACES

There is a lovely lazy mood here, so you should stay away if you want a place that is full of hustle and bustle. That is not to say that there is nothing to do; on the contrary, but it can be done at the pace you choose. The island of Lamu has been in a time warp for three hundred years. Since the Oman Sultan moved to Zanzibar, life has continued much as it was then. There are still no cars here; the narrow streets of the ancient town are very much as they were. One of the first trading outposts on the East African coast, it is a heady mix of Arab, Indian and African cultures. Classic boats common to this part of the world – dhows – still set sail each day as they have for centuries. There is a small family owned and run inn here, one that has long been a favorite escape of those in the know. Set on a headland, the Peponi Hotel is at a halfway point between two worlds. In one direction are the sounds and scenes of Lamu Old Town: white stone houses with intricately carved doorways, hidden courtyards, and tiny shops; and the haunting call to prayer from the mosques. In the other, a curve of beach – said to be crowded if ten people are on it – miles of white sand edged with turquoise water. You can sit and swing, rapt in a time zone of your own, look out at the Indian Ocean, sip a Lamu lime juice and question why you were ever in a rush. In Africa, it is said that "Even time takes its time." Robert Levine ◆ Books to pack: "Mr Bigstuff and the Goddess of Charm" by Fiona Sax Ledger; "A Geography of Time" by Robert Levine.

DIRECTIONS *A short boat ride from Lamu Town after a flight from Nairobi or Mombasa* · RATES *€€€* · ROOMS *29, all rooms have ocean views* · FOOD *The specialty is seafood, with ginger, lime and garlic – mangrove crabs, warm water lobster, squid, giant prawns and fish of all varieties. A Swahili menu is also available* · HISTORY *Opened in 1967, still owned and run by the same family* · X-FACTOR *At two degrees below the equator, there seems to be more time here*

# HANDELSAUSSENPOSTEN

Hier herrscht eine liebenswert faule Atmosphäre, und wenn Sie auf der Suche nach permanent geschäftigem Treiben sind, sollten Sie diesem Ort besser fernbleiben. Das heißt aber nicht, dass es hier nichts zu tun gäbe, im Gegenteil – aber die Geschwindigkeit, mit der Sie es tun, bestimmen Sie ganz einfach selbst. Seit nunmehr 300 Jahren befindet sich die Insel Lamu in einer Art Zeitschleife. Seitdem der Sultan von Oman nach Sansibar gezogen ist, hat das Leben hier ziemlich unverändert seinen Lauf genommen. Der erste Handelsaußenposten an der ostafrikanischen Küste ist eine eigenwillige Mischung aus arabischer, indischer und afrikanischer Kultur. Die traditionellen Boote, wie sie in diesem Teil der Welt üblich sind, die Dauen, setzen täglich ihre Segel, so wie sie es jahrhundertelang getan haben. Hier gibt es eine Pension in Familienbesitz, die schon seit langer Zeit der Lieblingszufluchtsort all jener ist, die das Glück haben, von ihrer Existenz zu wissen. Das Peponi Hotel, das auf einer Landzunge gelegen ist, markiert eine Art Scheidepunkt zwischen zwei Welten. Auf der einen Seite spielt sich das Leben von Lamus Altstadt mit all seinen typischen Geräuschen ab: weiße Steinhäuser mit aufwendig geschnitzten Eingangstüren, verborgenen Innenhöfen, winzige Läden, und der Aufruf zum Gebet schallt durchdringend von den Moscheen. Auf der anderen Seite der Strand – Meilen von weißem Sand begrenzt nur vom türkisfarbenen Wasser. Dieser Strand gilt übrigens als überfüllt, wenn sich mehr als zehn Menschen dort aufhalten. Hier kann man sitzen, die Seele baumeln lassen – in seine eigene Zeitzone entrückt –, während man auf den Indischen Ozean hinausblickt, Limettensaft aus Lamu schlürft und sich darüber wundert, warum man je so in Eile war. „In Afrika sagt man, dass sogar die Zeit ihre Zeit braucht." Robert Levine ◆ Buchtipps: „Eine Landkarte der Zeit. Wie Kulturen mit Zeit umgehen" von Robert Levine; „Nirgendwo in Afrika" von Stefanie Zweig.

**ANREISE** *Nach einem Flug von Nairobi oder Mombasa kurze Bootsfahrt von Lamu Town* · **PREIS** *€€€* · **ZIMMER** *29 Zimmer, alle mit Meeresblick* · **KÜCHE** *Spezialität des Hauses sind Fisch und Meeresfrüchte mit Ingwer und Knoblauch. Außerdem gibt es Swahili-Menüs* · **GESCHICHTE** *Eröffnet im Jahre 1967, seitdem im Besitz derselben Familie, die das Hotel auch führt* · **X-FAKTOR** *Zwei Grad unterhalb des Äquators scheint es einfach mehr Zeit zu geben*

# LE COMPTOIR OUBLIÉ

Il règne ici une ambiance délicieusement nonchalante. Si vous recherchez l'agitation et un tourbillon d'activité, cet endroit n'est pas pour vous. Cela ne veut dire pour autant qu'ici il n'y a rien à faire. Bien au contraire. Seulement, c'est vous qui décidez du rythme. Sur l'île de Lamu, le temps semble avoir suspendu son vol il y a trois cents ans. Depuis que le sultan d'Oman est parti pour Zanzibar, la vie n'a pratiquement pas changé. Il n'y a toujours pas de voitures, et les rues étroites de la vieille ville n'ont subi que peu de modifications. Lamu, l'un des premiers postes d'approvisionnement de la côte de l'Afrique orientale, est un mélange enivrant de culture arabe, indienne et africaine. Les boutres, embarcations typiques de cette partie du monde, prennent la mer tous les jours, et ce depuis des siècles. Lamu abrite une petite auberge familiale qu'affectionnent les rares privilégiés qui la connaissent. Dressé sur un promontoire, l'hôtel Peponi est à mi-chemin entre deux mondes : d'un côté, le spectacle et les sons du vieux Lamu, avec ses maisons en pierre blanche aux portes décorées de gravures complexes, ses cours cachées, ses minuscules échoppes et l'appel lancinant à la prière en provenance des mosquées ; de l'autre, une plage que les habitants jugent bondée dès que plus de dix personnes y posent le pied, et la mer turquoise bordée par des kilomètres de sable blanc. Vous pouvez vous asseoir, savourer le moment, et passer le temps, un temps qui n'appartient qu'à vous, à admirer l'océan Indien, en sirotant un jus de citron vert de Lamu et en vous demandant ce qui a bien pu vous obliger à vous presser par le passé. On dit en Afrique que « même le temps prend son temps ». Robert Levine ◆ À lire : « Une enfance africaine » de Stefanie Zweig ; « Les Swahili entre Afrique et Arabie » de Françoise Le Guennec-Coppens et Patricia Caplan.

**ACCÈS** *En avion jusqu'à Lamu depuis Nairobi ou Mombasa, puis court trajet en bateau* · **PRIX** *€€€* · **CHAMBRES** *29 chambres avec vue sur l'océan* · **RESTAURATION** *La spécialité de l'île sont les fruits de mer au gingembre, au citron vert et à l'ail : crabes de palétuvier, homards d'eau douce, calmars, crevettes géantes et poissons de toutes sortes. Un menu swahili est disponible* · **HISTOIRE** *Ouvert en 1967, l'hôtel appartient toujours à la même famille, qui le gère* · **LES « PLUS »** *Situé deux degrés en dessous de l'équateur, le temps semble s'écouler au ralenti*

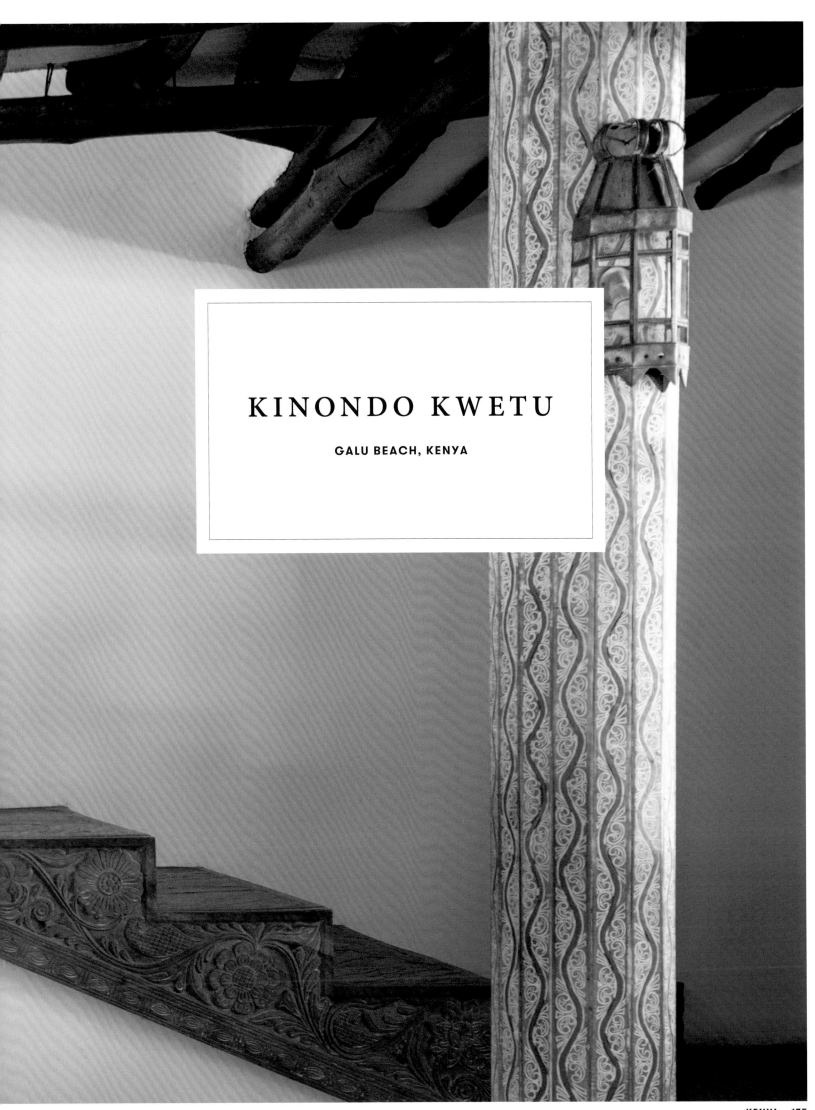

# KINONDO KWETU

**GALU BEACH, KENYA**

# KINONDO KWETU

Galu Beach, Kenya
Tel. +254 710 898 030 · info@kinondo-kwetu.com
www.kinondo-kwetu.com

## A SECOND HOME IN AFRICA

For the family of Ida Trygg and Filip Andersson, Kenya was a place where they longed to be as far back as the early twentieth century. At that time their best-known ancestors, Baron Blixen and his wife, moved south from Scandinavia. "Out of Africa" made their story into a legend. Ida and Filip have been living in Kenya with their children since 2005 – not on a coffee plantation in the highlands, like the Blixens, but right by the coast, on the Indian Ocean in a protected "kaya" region of sacred forests where the locals worship their ancestors. The couple have worked magic to turn an estate that once belonged to friends into a wonderful boutique lodge that has received multiple awards. It has cottages to which African craftwork lends charm, two pools, lots of hammocks and daybeds, as well as delicious food. Freshly caught fish, judiciously spiced vegetables and aromatic fruit are served in a changing series of favorite spots – in the shade of verandas and trees, beneath colorful sails, or on the beach in a decommissioned wooden boat. The beach, by the way, could feature in a travel brochure: it would be hard to find a more beautiful place to lie in white sand, gaze into turquoise waters, and dream the hours away. Guests who want to be active can go snorkeling, sailing, and surfing, or ride a horse by the ocean, and in Kinondo learn more about village life and the commitment shown by Ida and Filip. With money from their own fund they have set up a clinic in the village. They also support the nursery school and the primary school, and assist teenagers whose parents cannot afford more years of education. ◆ Book to pack: "Out of Africa" by Karen Blixen.

DIRECTIONS *In a very quiet location on Galu Beach in 6.5 hectares/ 16 acres of grounds. The nearest hotel is just 2 km/over 1 mile away. To the airstrip at Ukunda it takes 15–20 minutes by car, to Mombasa international airport 1.5–2 hours ·* RATES *€€€€; including full board (with beer and the house wine) and many leisure activities ·* ROOMS *5 cottages with 1–3 bedrooms, 1 villa with 2 bedrooms, 1 villa with 8 suites (for exclusive booking or room by room), 1 holiday house with 4 bedrooms, living area and kitchenette ·* FOOD *Dishes made from organic local produce and inspired by the east coast of Africa. There are fixed menus at midday and in the evening, but the chef also caters for individual wishes ·* HISTORY *Filip's parents bought the estate in 2004. Ida and Filip acquired the surrounding land, opened the hotel in 2005, and extended it up to 2008, when the clinic too was opened ·* X-FACTOR *Kinondo Kwetu can be booked exclusively, for example for weddings or yoga retreats*

# ZWEITE HEIMAT AFRIKA

Für die Familie von Ida Trygg und Filip Andersson war Kenia schon Anfang des 20. Jahrhunderts ein Sehnsuchtsziel: Damals reisten ihre berühmtesten Vorfahren, Baron Blixen und seine Frau, von Skandinavien aus in den Süden. Ihre Geschichte wurde dank „Jenseits von Afrika" zur Legende. Ida und Filip leben mit ihren Kindern seit 2005 in Kenia – nicht auf einer Kaffeeplantage im Hochland wie die Blixens, sondern an der Küste, direkt am Indischen Ozean und in einem geschützten „Kaya"-Gebiet mit heiligen Wäldern, in denen die Einheimischen ihre Ahnen verehren. Aus einem Anwesen, das einst Freunden gehörte, hat das Paar eine wunderbare und mehrfach preisgekrönte Boutiquelodge gezaubert. Mit Cottages, denen afrikanisches Kunsthandwerk Charme verleiht, zwei Pools, jeder Menge Hängematten und Daybeds sowie köstlicher Küche. Fangfrischer Fisch, fein gewürztes Gemüse und duftendes Obst werden an wechselnden Lieblingsplätzen serviert – im Schatten der Veranden und Bäume, unter bunten Segeln oder in einem ausrangierten Holzboot am Strand. Dieser fällt übrigens in die Kategorie Bilderbuchbeach: Auf dem weißen Sand zu liegen, aufs türkisblaue Wasser zu schauen und in den Tag hineinzuträumen, ist selten schöner als hier. Wer aktiv sein will, kann schnorcheln, segeln und surfen, am Meer entlangreiten oder in Kinondo mehr über das dörfliche Leben und das Engagement von Ida und Filip erfahren. Mit Geldern aus ihrem eigenen Fonds haben die beiden im Ort eine Klinik aufgebaut, unterstützen den Kindergarten sowie die Grundschule und fördern Teenager, deren Eltern weiterführende Bildung nicht bezahlen können. ◆ Buchtipp: „Jenseits von Afrika" von Tania Blixen.

**ANREISE** *Sehr ruhig am Galu Beach auf einem 6,5 Hektar großen Grundstück gelegen, das nächste Hotel ist 2 km entfernt. Zum Flugplatz Ukunda fährt man 15–20 Min., zum internationalen Flughafen Mombasa 1,5–2 Std.* · **PREIS** *€€€€; inkl. Vollpension (mit Bier und Hauswein) und zahlreichen Freizeitangeboten* · **ZIMMER** *5 Cottages mit 1–3 Zimmern, 1 Villa mit 2 Zimmern, 1 Villa mit 8 Suiten (exklusiv oder zimmerweise zu vermieten), 1 Ferienhaus mit 4 Zimmern, Wohnbereich sowie Kitchenette* · **KÜCHE** *Von der afrikanischen Ostküste inspirierte Gerichte aus lokalen Biozutaten. Mittags und abends gibt es fixe Menüs, der Koch erfüllt aber auch individuelle Wünsche* · **GESCHICHTE** *Filips Eltern kauften das Anwesen 2004. Ida und Filip erwarben das umliegende Land, eröffneten das Hotel 2005 und erweiterten es bis 2008. In dem Jahr entstand auch die Klinik* · **X-FAKTOR** *Kinondo Kwetu kann exklusiv, z. B. für Hochzeiten oder Yoga-Retreats, gebucht werden*

# AFRIQUE, L'AUTRE TERRE-MÈRE

Le Kenya fascinait déjà la famille d'Ida Trygg et de Filip Andersson au début du XXᵉ siècle – c'est à cette époque que leurs ancêtres les plus célèbres, le baron Blixen et sa femme, ont quitté la Scandinavie pour l'Afrique orientale. Leur histoire est devenue légendaire grâce au roman « La ferme africaine ». Ida et Filip vivent avec leurs enfants au Kenya depuis 2005 – pas dans une plantation de café sur les hauts plateaux comme les Blixen, mais sur la côte, au bord de l'océan Indien, et dans une zone protégée « Kaya » abritant des forêts sacrées où les autochtones vénèrent leurs ancêtres. Le couple a transformé une propriété qui appartenait autrefois à des amis en un magnifique lodge-boutique, plusieurs fois primé. On y trouve des cottages, auxquels l'artisanat africain confère beaucoup de charme, deux piscines, une multitude de hamacs et de lits de repos ainsi qu'une cuisine exquise. Le poisson qui vient d'être pêché, les légumes subtilement assaisonnés et les fruits parfumés sont servis dans divers lieux de prédilection – à l'ombre des vérandas et des arbres, sous des voiles aux vives couleurs ou dans un bateau en bois abandonné sur la plage. Celle-ci semble tout droit sortie d'un livre d'images : s'allonger sur le sable blanc, regarder l'eau turquoise et rêver… difficile de trouver un endroit plus approprié. Les amateurs de sport et d'activités peuvent faire du snorkeling, de la voile et du surf, se promener à cheval sur le rivage ou s'intéresser à la vie du village et à l'engagement d'Ida et de Filip qui, avec l'argent de leur propre fonds, ont construit une clinique à Kinondo, apportent leur soutien au jardin d'enfants et à l'école primaire et aident les adolescents dont les parents ne peuvent pas payer l'enseignement secondaire. ◆ À lire : « La ferme africaine » de Karen Blixen.

**ACCÈS** *Situé dans un endroit calme sur la plage de Galu sur un terrain de 6,5 hectares, l'hôtel le plus proche est à 2 km. L'aéroport d'Ukunda est à 15–20 min de route, l'aéroport international de Mombasa à 1,5–2 h* · **PRIX** *€€€€; pension complète (avec bière et vin maison) incluse et de nombreuses activités de loisirs* · **CHAMBRES** *5 cottages de 1 à 3 chambres, 1 villa de 2 chambres, 1 villa de 8 suites (à louer en exclusivité ou par chambre), 1 maison de vacances de 4 chambres avec séjour et kitchenette* · **RESTAURATION** *Des plats inspirés de la côte est-africaine, préparés avec des produits locaux issus de l'agriculture biologique. Des menus fixes sont proposés pour le déjeuner et le dîner, mais le chef répond également aux souhaits individuels* · **HISTOIRE** *Les parents de Filip ont acquis la propriété en 2004. Ida et Filip ont acheté les terrains environnants, ouvert l'hôtel en 2005 et l'ont agrandi jusqu'en 2008. La clinique a également été créée cette année-là* · **LES « PLUS »** *Kinondo Kwetu peut être réservé en exclusivité, par exemple pour des mariages ou des retraites de yoga*

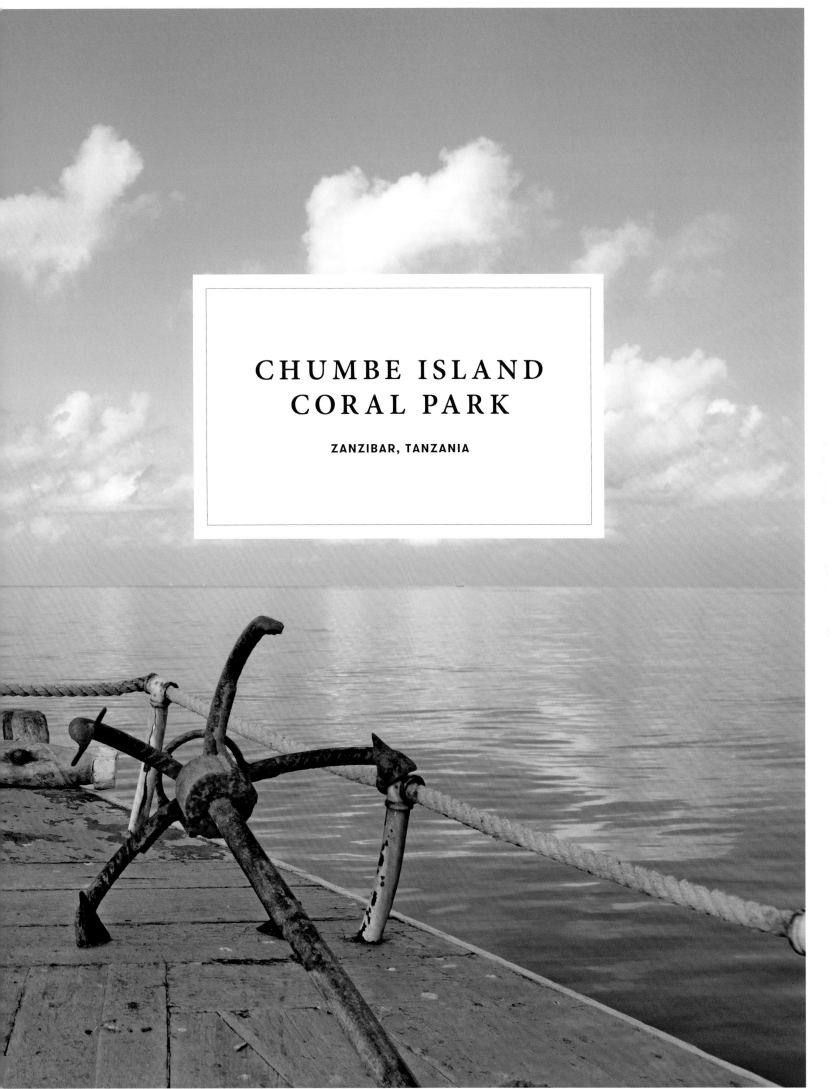

# CHUMBE ISLAND
# CORAL PARK

## ZANZIBAR, TANZANIA

# CHUMBE ISLAND CORAL PARK

P.O. Box 3203, Zanzibar, Tanzania
Tel. +255 24 223 10 40 · book@chumbeisland.com
www.chumbeisland.com

## BAREFOOT LUXURY

Rising up on a small island between Zanzibar and Dar es Salaam is a lighthouse. Its flashing beam guides the dhows, boats that have crossed this sea for a thousand years. The tower also signals the location of one of the most spectacular coral gardens on earth. Beneath the water, corals in a kaleidoscope of colors teem with fish. Chumbe Island Coral Park is a private nature reserve, covered by an evergreen forest. This is an ecological sanctuary where the rare duiker antelope roam and giant coconut crabs climb to the top of trees in search of food. Few other buildings, or people, are here. Soaring thatched roofs amongst the foliage mark the existence of just seven bungalows. Water and energy are provided by nature, and they have solar-powered lights and hot water. All face the turquoise-blue ocean, and it takes just a few seconds to stroll to the beach and reef. Or you can just look at it, lying in your comfortable hammock. This is rather like camping out, but in comparative luxury, and sleeping, dreaming, under a palm-thatched roof.
◆ Book to pack: "Robinson Crusoe" by Daniel Defoe.

DIRECTIONS *Fly to Zanzibar, take a boat from the beach at the Mbweni Ruins hotel* · RATES *€€€* · ROOMS *7 sustainably built bungalows* · FOOD *Dishes typical of the island, combining Arab, Indian and African aromas* · HISTORY *The Government of Zanzibar declared it a closed forest in 1994, and the management was entrusted to the Chumbe Island Coral Park, an autonomous organisation* · X-FACTOR *Castaway in style*

## DER LUXUS, BARFUSS ZU LAUFEN

Auf einer kleinen Insel zwischen Sansibar und Daressalam steht ein Leuchtturm. Sein blinkender Lichtstrahl weist den Dauen – Booten, die schon seit 1000 Jahren durch dieses Meer segeln – die Richtung. Der Leuchtturm weist auch den Weg zu einem der eindrucksvollsten Korallenriffe der Welt. In den Tiefen des Meeres kann man hier inmitten der bunten Farbenpracht der Korallen ganze Schwärme von Fischen bewundern. Chumbe Island Coral Park ist ein privater Naturschutzpark, der von einem immergrünen Wald überzogen ist, ein ökologisches Heiligtum, in dem die seltene Duiker-Antilope frei umherstreift und Riesenkokosnusskrabben bei ihrer Nahrungssuche in die Baumkronen hinaufklettern. Sonst gibt es hier wenig andere Gebäude oder Menschen. An den strohgedeckten Dächern, die aus den Blättern ragen, lässt sich erkennen, dass es hier nicht mehr als sieben Bungalows gibt. Wasser und Strom liefert die Natur, die Bungalows haben solarbetriebenes Licht und heißes Wasser und sind alle auf das türkisblaue Meer hin ausgerichtet. Mit nur wenigen Schritten gelangt man an den Strand und das Riff. Oder man genießt einfach nur deren Anblick, während man in seiner bequemen Hängematte liegt. Das Ganze erinnert eher an Camping, aber mit vergleichsweise hohem Luxus; schlafen und träumen unterm Palmendach. ◆ Buchtipp: „Robinson Crusoe" von Daniel Defoe.

**ANREISE** *Fliegen Sie nach Sansibar, vom Strand des Mbweni Ruins Hotel aus nehmen Sie ein Boot ·* **PREIS** *€€€ ·* **ZIMMER** *7 nachhaltig erbaute Bungalows ·* **KÜCHE** *Inseltypische Gerichte, die arabische, indische und afrikanische Aromen verbinden ·* **GESCHICHTE** *Im Jahre 1994 wurde der Wald von der Regierung Sansibars unter Naturschutz gestellt und die Verwaltung Chumbe Island Coral Park anvertraut, einer selbsttragenden Organisation ·* **X-FAKTOR** *Romantische Einsamkeit*

## LES PIEDS NUS DANS LE LUXE

Sur une petite île entre Zanzibar et Dar es Salaam se dresse un phare. Son faisceau lumineux guide les boutres, des bateaux qui traversent l'océan depuis un millier d'années. Cette tour indique également la présence de l'un des jardins de corail les plus spectaculaires du monde. Sous l'eau, les coraux aux couleurs éclatantes foisonnent de poissons. Chumbe Island Coral Park est une réserve naturelle privée recouverte d'une forêt à feuillage persistant. Dans ce sanctuaire écologique, les céphalophes, antilopes rares, s'ébattent en toute liberté et les crabes géants de cocotier grimpent au sommet des arbres à la recherche de nourriture. Il n'y a guère d'autres constructions, et la solitude règne. Des toits hauts et couverts de chaume dépassant du feuillage marquent la présence de sept bungalows seulement. L'eau est fournie par la nature et chauffée grâce à l'énergie solaire qui assure également l'éclairage. Tous les bungalows donnent sur l'océan bleu turquoise, et la plage et les récifs ne sont qu'à quelques secondes à pied. Bien sûr, vous pouvez aussi vous contenter de les observer de loin, confortablement installé dans votre hamac. Vous aurez l'impression de camper, mais dans un camping de luxe, et vous dormirez et rêverez sous un toit recouvert de palmes. ◆ À lire : « Robinson Crusoé » de Daniel Defoe.

**ACCÈS** *Après un vol jusqu'à Zanzibar, le bateau se prend sur la plage de l'hôtel Mbweni Ruins ·* **PRIX** *€€€ ·* **CHAMBRES** *7 bungalows construits en matériaux naturels et durables ·* **RESTAURATION** *Cuisine typique de Zanzibar qui marie les saveurs arabes, indiennes et africaines ·* **HISTOIRE** *La forêt de l'île a été décrétée forêt protégée par le gouvernement de Zanzibar en 1994, et sa gestion a été confiée au Chumbe Island Coral Park, une organisation indépendante ·* **LES « PLUS »** *Isolement et style*

# GIBB'S FARM

KARATU, NEAR ARUSHA, TANZANIA

VEG TEBLE
Leeks          H
Carrots        Min
Beatroot       Thyr
Lettuce        Coria
White Cabb.    Arag
Red Cabbage    Rosen
Green Pepper   Chi
Squash         Dill
Broccol        Fe
Spirnach
Cucumber       S
Turnips
Kay

# GIBB'S FARM

P.O. Box 280, Karatu, near Arusha, Tanzania
Tel. +255 272 970 436 and +255 272 970 438 · reservations@gibbsfarm.com
www.gibbsfarm.com

## ON THE COFFEE PLANTATION

Coffee has been known in Tanzania since the 16th century, when the Haya people are said to have introduced an early variety from Ethiopia. It was firmly established by Catholic missionaries in the late 19th century, and coffee cultivation is now one of the leading sectors of the Tanzanian economy. The most popular kind is the aromatic Arabica bean, which is grown on Gibb's Farm. A German aristocrat founded the estate in 1929 and reported proudly that he had built a "cool, rain-proof and friendly" main house. It was also robust, as it is still standing, and today accommodates the cosy living and dining rooms of the farm. After the Second World War, the British veteran James Gibb took over the plantation, and in the early 1970s opened one of the first guesthouses in northern Tanzania with his wife Margaret. Since then it has never lost its rustic, luxurious charm: the individually equipped cottages have floors of eucalyptus wood, hand-made furniture, indoor and outdoor showers, and exhibit works by Tanzanian and international artists, who come here to take part in an artist-in-residence program. The house is surrounded by a blooming garden, a source of ingredients for the hotel kitchen, and the four-hectare coffee plantation. To watch the beans being roasted and then to enjoy a cup of freshly brewed coffee is a treat for all of the senses – a taste of Africa. ◆ Book to pack: "Liberty" by Jakob Ejersbo.

DIRECTIONS *In Karatu, near the Ngorongoro Crater. 35 minutes from the airstrip at Lake Manyara, 2.5 hours from Arusha airport ·* RATES *€€€–€€€€; with half or full board ·* ROOMS *17 cottages (2 of them for 4 persons) ·* FOOD *Fresh country cooking with ingredients from the hotel's own organic farm – and delicious coffee, of course! ·* HISTORY *Opened in 1972 as a hotel, and extended several times since then ·* X-FACTOR *Spa treatments based on traditional healing methods of the Masai*

# AUF DER KAFFEEPLANTAGE

Kaffee kennt man in Tansania schon seit dem 16. Jahrhundert – damals soll das Volk der Haya eine frühe Sorte aus Äthiopien ins Land gebracht haben. Fest etabliert haben ihn katholische Missionare Ende des 19. Jahrhunderts, und inzwischen zählt der Kaffeeanbau zu den wichtigsten Wirtschaftszweigen Tansanias. Am populärsten ist die aromatische Arabica-Bohne, die auch auf Gibb's Farm kultiviert wird. Ein deutscher Freiherr begründete das Anwesen 1929 und berichtete damals stolz, ein „kühles, regenfestes und freundliches" Haupthaus errichtet zu haben. Stabil war es zudem, denn es steht noch immer und beherbergt heute die gemütlichen Wohn- sowie Esszimmer der Farm. Nach dem Zweiten Weltkrieg erwarb der britische Veteran James Gibb die Plantage und eröffnete gemeinsam mit seiner Frau Margaret Anfang der 1970er eines der ersten Gasthäuser im Norden von Tansania. Den rustikal-luxuriösen Charme hat es sich seither immer erhalten: Die individuell eingerichteten Cottages sind mit Böden aus Eukalyptusholz, handgefertigten Möbeln sowie Innen- und Außenduschen ausgestattet und zeigen Werke einheimischer und internationaler Künstler, die im Rahmen eines „Artist-in-Residence"-Programms hierherkommen. Rund um die Häuser liegen ein blühender Garten, der Quell für die Hotelküche ist, sowie die vier Hektar große Kaffeeplantage. Beim Rösten der Bohnen zuzusehen und anschließend eine Tasse frisch aufgebrühten Kaffee zu genießen, ist ein Erlebnis für alle Sinne – so schmeckt Afrika. ◆ Buchtipp: „Liberty" von Jakob Ejersbo.

**ANREISE** *In Karatu nahe des Ngorongoro-Kraters gelegen. 35 Min. vom Flugplatz Lake Manyara, 2,5 Std. vom Flughafen Arusha entfernt ·* **PREIS** *€€€–€€€€; mit Halb- oder Vollpension ·* **ZIMMER** *17 Cottages (davon 2 für 4 Personen) ·* **KÜCHE** *Frische Landküche mit Zutaten aus eigenem, organischem Anbau – und natürlich köstlicher Kaffee! ·* **GESCHICHTE** *1972 als Hotel eröffnet und seither mehrmals erweitert ·* **X-FAKTOR** *Die Spa-Anwendungen, die auf traditionellen Heilmethoden der Massai basieren*

# DANS LA CAFÉIÈRE

Le café est connu en Tanzanie depuis le XVIe siècle – à l'époque, le peuple Haya aurait introduit dans le pays une variété précoce originaire d'Éthiopie. Il a été fermement établi par des missionnaires catholiques à la fin du XIXe siècle, et la culture du café est aujourd'hui l'un des secteurs économiques les plus importants de la Tanzanie. Le plus populaire est le type arabica, d'une grande finesse aromatique, qui est également cultivé à Gibb's Farm. Le baron allemand qui a fondé le domaine en 1929 racontait avec fierté qu'il avait construit une maison principale « fraîche, imperméable et conviviale ». Elle était également stable, vu qu'elle existe encore et abrite aujourd'hui le salon confortable et la salle à manger de la ferme. Après la Seconde Guerre mondiale, l'ancien combattant britannique James Gibb a acquis la plantation et a ouvert au début des années 1970 avec son épouse Margaret l'une des premières maisons d'hôtes dans le nord de la Tanzanie. Le charme à la fois rustique et luxueux a été préservé : les cottages aménagés individuellement ont des planchers en bois d'eucalyptus, sont équipés de meubles faits à la main et de douches intérieures et extérieures, et abritent des œuvres d'artistes locaux et internationaux qui viennent ici dans le cadre d'un programme d'« artistes en résidence ». Les maisons sont entourées d'un jardin fleuri qui ravitaille la cuisine de l'hôtel, et d'une plantation de café de quatre hectares. Observer la torréfaction et déguster une tasse de café fraîchement préparé est une expérience qui fait appel aux cinq sens – c'est le goût de l'Afrique. ◆ À lire : « Liberty » de Jakob Ejersbo.

**ACCÈS** *Situé à Karatu à proximité du cratère du Ngorongoro. À 35 min de l'aérodrome Lake Manyara, à 2 h 30 de l'aéroport d'Arusha ·* **PRIX** *€€€–€€€€; avec demi-pension ou pension complète ·* **CHAMBRES** *17 cottages (dont 2 pour 4 personnes) ·* **RESTAURATION** *Cuisine rustique à base d'ingrédients bio produits ici – sans oublier le délicieux café ! ·* **HISTOIRE** *L'hôtel a ouvert ses portes en 1972 et a été agrandi plusieurs fois depuis ·* **LES « PLUS »** *Les soins Spa basés sur des méthodes de traitement traditionnelles des Massaï*

# TARANGIRE
# TREETOPS

TARANGIRE CONSERVATION AREA, TANZANIA

# TARANGIRE TREETOPS

Tarangire Conservation Area, Tanzania
Tel. +255 754 250 630 and +255 784 250 630 · reservations@elewana.com
www.elewanacollection.com

## BAOBAB BUNGALOWS

The baobab tree is one of the most stunning sights in Africa. It can grow to a massive size; some are hundreds of years old. In many parts of the continent it is thought to be sacred. Legend has it that the tree so angered the gods that they tore it up then flung it back to earth, upside down, so it landed with its roots in the air. The chalets that make up Tarangire Treetops Lodge are built on platforms high up in the canopy of these extraordinary trees. When we were children many of us fell in love with tree houses; sometimes we fell head over heels out of them. We had to give them up when we grew up. The tree houses here are far more sophisticated than our childish kind; they may be among trees but that is where the resemblance ends – and all for the better. These are definitely a step up, and more. A bar is set among the eaves of a massive baobab, where drinks are served before dinner. Even the dining "room" is built around a tree. And the creators of the Lodge really "branched out" in their design of the chalets; each 65-square-meter tree house includes a bedroom as well as a deluxe bathroom. The décor is stylish too, a skillful mix of local fabrics, Masai craftsmanship and Swahili opulence. Down at ground level are the neighbors. Leopard, cheetah, lion, greater kudu and huge herds of elephant are at home here.
◆ Book to pack: "The Flame Trees of Thika: Memories of an African Childhood" by Elspeth Huxley.

**DIRECTIONS** *120 km/75 miles south-west of Arusha, or by plane 20 minutes from Arusha (airstrip in Kuro)* · **RATES** *€€€€* · **ROOMS** *20 tree huts with a view of baobab and maroela trees* · **FOOD** *Old world cuisine simmered in the African melting pot* · **HISTORY** *The lodge was built with the local Masai community* · **X-FACTOR** *A chance to re-live childhood days*

# BAOBAB-BUNGALOWS

Der Affenbrotbaum gehört zu den verblüffendsten Sehenswürdigkeiten Afrikas. Er kann zu einer enormen Größe heranwachsen und manche Exemplare sind mehrere Hundert Jahre alt. In vielen Teilen des Kontinents gilt der Baobab als heilig. Eine Legende besagt, dass der Baum die Götter so sehr ärgerte, dass sie ihn zerfetzten und ihn mit der Krone nach unten zurück auf die Erde warfen, sodass er mit den Wurzeln nach oben landete. Die Hütten, aus denen sich Tarangire Treetops Lodge zusammensetzt, wurden auf Plattformen gebaut, die hoch oben zwischen diesen Bäumen thronen. Kopfüber haben sich viele von uns als Kinder in die Idee verliebt, ein Baumhaus zu haben, kopfüber ist so mancher hinuntergefallen, und als wir älter wurden, mussten wir sie aufgeben. Diese Baumhäuser hier sind von technisch viel raffinierterer Art, als es unsere „kindlichen" Baumhäuser waren. Zwar befinden sie sich zwischen Bäumen, doch damit endet die Ähnlichkeit auch schon, denn sie sind definitiv viel ausgeklügelter. Wer möchte, kann vor dem Abendessen einen Drink an der Bar einnehmen, die zwischen die Stämme eines riesigen Affenbrotbaumes gebaut wurde. Selbst der „Speisesaal" ist um einen Baum gebaut. Und was die Inneneinrichtung der Hütten angeht, kann man nur sagen, dass die Gestalter der Lodge „astrein" geplant haben. Jedes Baumhaus umfasst ein Schlafzimmer sowie ein Luxusbadezimmer und ist 65 Quadratmeter groß. Der Dekor ist ebenfalls stilvoll – eine gekonnte Mischung aus einheimischen Materialien, Massai-Handwerkskunst und opulenter Swahili-Kunst. Unten am Grund leben die Nachbarn. Hier sind Leopard, Gepard, Löwe, die große Kudu-Antilope und riesige Elefantenherden zu Hause. ◆ Buchtipp: „Die Flammenbäume von Thika. Erinnerungen an eine Kindheit in Afrika" von Elspeth Huxley.

**ANREISE** *Mit dem Flugzeug 20 Min. von Arusha (gelandet wird in Kuro)* · **PREIS** *€€€€* · **ZIMMER** *20 Baumhütten mit Blick auf Affenbrot- und Maroelabäume* · **KÜCHE** *Europäische Küche mit afrikanischem Einschlag* · **GESCHICHTE** *Die Lodge wurde zusammen mit den einheimischen Massai gebaut* · **X-FAKTOR** *Lassen Sie sich in Ihre Kindheit zurückversetzen*

# BAOBAB BUNGALOWS

Le baobab est l'un des arbres les plus fascinants d'Afrique. Considéré comme sacré dans de nombreuses régions du continent, il peut atteindre des hauteurs vertigineuses et certains spécimens sont plusieurs fois centenaires. La légende dit que son aspect vient de ce que les dieux, courroucés par son gigantisme, le déracinèrent et le renvoyèrent sur terre, tête en bas et racines en l'air. Les bungalows de Tarangire Treetops Lodge sont érigés sur des plates-formes installées dans la voûte de ces arbres extraordinaires. Enfants, nombre d'entre nous étaient friands des cabanes construites dans les arbres. Certains même les trouvaient si bien qu'ils en tombaient parfois à la renverse. En grandissant, nous avons dû y renoncer. Les « cabanes » de Tarangire Treetops sont bien plus sophistiquées que celles de notre enfance. Elles sont installées parmi les arbres, soit, mais la ressemblance s'arrête là, ce qui est tout à votre avantage. Ces cabanes sont d'une catégorie bien supérieure. Un bar installé entre les feuilles d'un énorme baobab vous attend pour un apéritif avant le dîner et même la salle du restaurant accueille un arbre en son centre. Par ailleurs, les créateurs de l'hôtel ont exploré une branche réellement originale de la conception de bungalows. D'une surface de 65 mètres carrés, chacune de ces cabanes dans les arbres comprend une chambre et est équipée d'une salle de bains luxueuse. La décoration, tout aussi élégante, est une habile combinaison d'étoffes locales, d'artisanat massaï et d'opulence swahili. Les voisins habitent au rez-de-chaussée : léopards, guépards, lions, grands kudus et énormes troupeaux d'éléphants sont ici chez eux. ◆ À lire : « Le lion » de Joseph Kessel.

**ACCÈS** *En voiture, à 120 km au sud-ouest d'Arusha, ou par avion à 20 min d'Arusha (atterrissage à Kuro)* · **PRIX** *€€€€* · **CHAMBRES** *20 cabanes dans les arbres avec vue sur les baobabs et les marulas* · **RESTAURATION** *Cuisine européenne aux saveurs africaines* · **HISTOIRE** *Hôtel construit avec les Massaï* · **LES « PLUS »** *L'occasion de redevenir enfant*

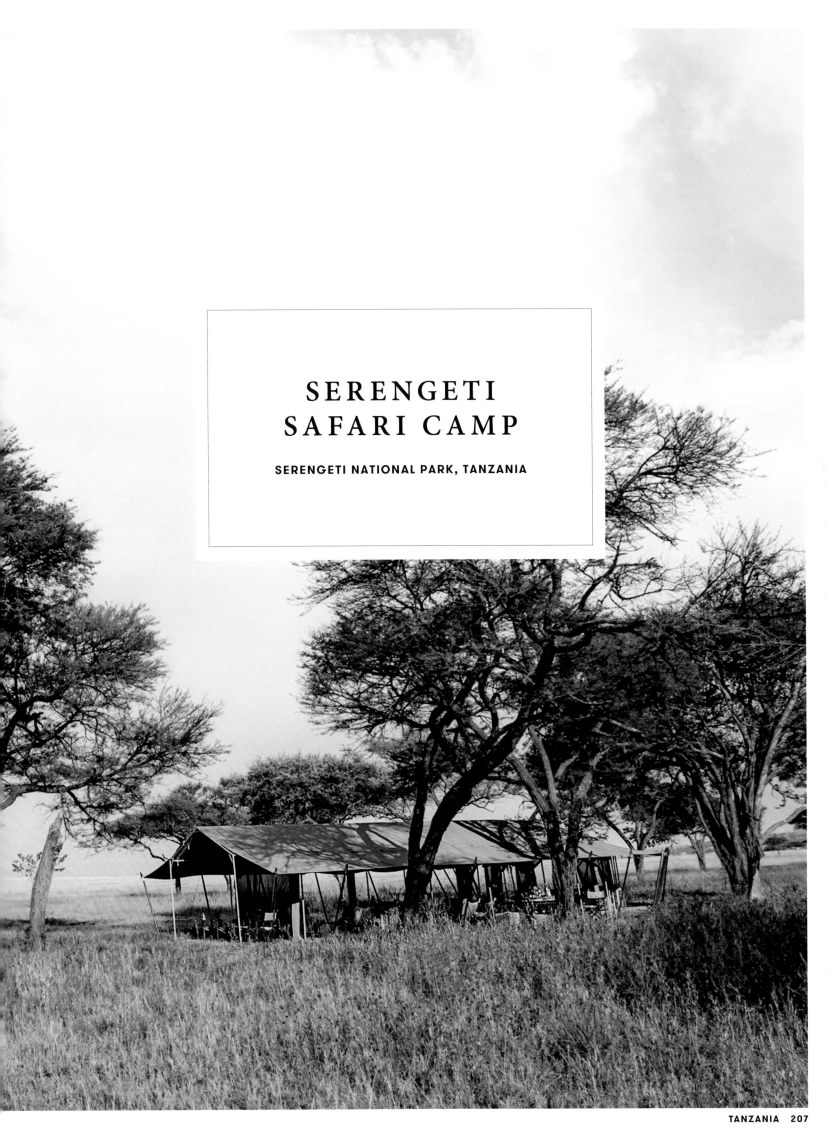

# SERENGETI
# SAFARI CAMP

### SERENGETI NATIONAL PARK, TANZANIA

# SERENGETI SAFARI CAMP

Nomad Tanzania, Tanzania
Tel. +255 787 595 908 · info@nomad-tanzania.com
www.nomad-tanzania.com

## AFRICA CLOSE-UP

A herd of zebras grazing in the shade of bizarrely shaped trees. A family of leopards, lazing in the grass one moment and chasing off at top speed only a few seconds later. Scores of gnus, plowing dramatically through foaming, grey-brown river water. Hardly anywhere else can you get as close to Africa as here, feel the fascination of the continent so directly, and see more million-dollar motifs than even Instagram could ever handle. The Serengeti Safari Camp is mobile, following the migrations of wildlife all year round – from the Ndutu region in the south of the Serengeti, where animals give birth to their young, to the Seronera valley with its seemingly infinite plains, and the river Grumeti, where crocodiles command respect. Re-erected every few months, the camp consists of just a handful of tents, which are equipped extremely comfortably in the safari style – including private bathrooms with ecological toilets and bucket showers, which can be filled with warm water on request. During the day, supervised by experienced guides, guests follow the tracks of the Serengeti's residents in four-wheel-drive vehicles, and in the evenings meals are taken together in the main tent, with stories of Africa around the camp fire. As the Serengeti calls on the senses all round the clock, it sometimes takes a while to get to sleep, as the calls and movements of animals can be heard around the tents. But at sunrise, you can be sure that adrenalin will dispel any tiredness. ◆ Book to pack: "Lioness" by Katherine Scholes.

DIRECTIONS *The location of the camp changes with the seasons. Travel guides pick up participants in the safari at central points, e.g. at a hotel or the airport in Arusha ·* RATES *€€€€; including the complete safari package ·* ROOMS *6 tents for 2 persons, 1 family tent with 2 sleeping areas (children from the age of 8 welcome) ·* FOOD *All meals are freshly prepared on the spot and served in the tent or in the open air. There is even a separate bar tent ·* HISTORY *For 20 years, Nomad Tanzania has been organizing safaris to remote, less-known parts of the country ·* X-FACTOR *More nature and wildlife is not possible*

# AFRIKA AUS NÄCHSTER NÄHE

Eine Herde Zebras, die im Schatten skurril geformter Bäume weidet. Eine Gepardenfamilie, die eben noch faul im Gras liegt und nur Sekunden später in Höchstgeschwingkeit davonjagt. Eine Hundertschaft Gnus, die dramatisch durchs graubraun schäumende Flusswasser pflügt: Kaum irgendwo sonst kommt man Afrika so nahe wie hier, spürt die Faszination dieses Kontinents so unmittelbar und sieht mehr „Million Dollar"-Motive als selbst Instagram jemals fassen könnte: Das Serengeti Safari Camp ist mobil und folgt das ganze Jahr über der Wanderung der Wildtiere – vom Ndutu-Gebiet im Süden der Serengeti, wo die Tiere ihren Nachwuchs zur Welt bringen, über das Seronera-Tal mit seinen unendlich erscheinenden Ebenen bis zum Fluss Grumeti, in dem Respekt einflößende Krokodile hausen. Alle paar Monate neu aufgebaut, besteht das Camp nur aus einer Handvoll Zelten, die äußerst komfortabel im Safaristil ausgestattet sind – inklusive privaten Bädern mit Ökotoilette und Eimerdusche, in die auf Wunsch sogar warmes Wasser gefüllt wird. Tagsüber und unter Leitung erfahrener Führer folgen die Gäste im Allradwagen den Spuren der Serengetibewohner, abends gibt es im Hauptzelt eine gemeinsame Mahlzeit und am offenen Feuer Geschichten über Afrika. Da die Serengeti die Sinne rund um die Uhr fordert, lässt der Schlaf unter Umständen auf sich warten, da man rings um die Zelte Tiertrappeln und -stimmen hört. Doch bei Sonnenaufgang vertreibt das Adrenalin mit Sicherheit die Müdigkeit. ◆ Buchtipp: „Das Herz einer Löwin" von Katherine Scholes.

ANREISE *Je nach Jahreszeit wechseln die Standorte des Camps. Die Reiseleiter holen die Safariteilnehmer an zentralen Treffpunkten ab, z. B. am Hotel oder Flughafen in Arusha ·* PREIS *€€€€; inklusive des kompletten Safari-Packages ·* ZIMMER *6 Zelte für 2 Personen, 1 Familienzelt mit 2 Schlafbereichen (Kinder sind ab 8 Jahren willkommen) ·* KÜCHE *Alle Mahlzeiten werden frisch vor Ort zubereitet und im Zelt oder unter freiem Himmel serviert. Es gibt sogar ein eigenes Bar-Zelt ·* GESCHICHTE *Seit 20 Jahren organisiert Nomad Tanzania Safaris in entlegeneren, unbekannteren Teilen des Landes ·* X-FAKTOR *Mehr Natur und „Wildlife" geht nicht*

# L'AFRIQUE AU PLUS PRÈS

Un troupeau de zèbres broutant à l'ombre d'arbres aux formes singulières. Une famille de guépards paresseusement allongés dans l'herbe et qui s'enfuit à toute allure quelques secondes plus tard. Une centaine de gnous qui sillonnent de manière alarmante les eaux gris-brun bouillonnantes de la rivière : nulle part ailleurs on ne peut se sentir aussi proche de l'Afrique, subir l'attrait irrésistible de ce continent de manière aussi directe et voir plus de motifs époustouflants que même Instagram ne pourrait en poster : le Serengeti Safari Camp est mobile et suit la migration des animaux sauvages tout au long de l'année – de la région de Ndutu au sud du Serengeti, où les femelles donnent naissance à leurs petits, en traversant la vallée de Seronera et ses plaines apparemment infinies, jusqu'à la rivière Grumeti, où vivent des crocodiles qui inspirent le respect. Reconstruit tous les quelques mois, le camp ne comporte que quelques tentes, toutes très confortablement équipées dans le style safari – y compris des salles de bains privées avec toilettes écologiques et douches à seau (ils peuvent être remplis d'eau chaude sur demande). Pendant la journée et sous la direction de guides expérimentés, les participants suivent les traces des habitants du Serengeti dans le véhicule tout-terrain, prennent le soir un repas commun dans la tente principale et écoutent des histoires sur l'Afrique racontées près d'un feu de camp. Comme le Serengeti sollicite les sens 24 heures sur 24, le sommeil peut être long à venir, car on entend les bruits et les cris des animaux évoluant autour des tentes. Mais au lever du soleil, l'adrénaline chassera certainement la fatigue. ◆ À lire : « La lionne » de Katherine Scholes.

ACCÈS *L'emplacement du camp change selon la saison. Les guides vont chercher les participants à des points de rencontre, par exemple l'hôtel ou l'aéroport à Arusha ·* PRIX *€€€€; packages safari inclus ·* CHAMBRES *6 tentes à 2 personnes, 1 tente familiale avec zones de couchage (les enfants sont bienvenus à partir de 8 ans) ·* RESTAURATION *Tous les repas sont préparés sur place et servis sous la tente ou en plein air. Il y a même une tente-bar ·* HISTOIRE *Nomad Tanzania organise depuis 20 ans des safaris dans des parties reculées, inconnues du pays ·* LES « PLUS » *Impossible de trouver plus de nature et de vie sauvage*

# FREGATE ISLAND PRIVATE

## FRÉGATE ISLAND, SEYCHELLES

# FREGATE ISLAND PRIVATE

Frégate Island, Seychelles
Tel. +248 4397 100 and +49 69 247 549 400 · reservations@fregatetravel.com
www.fregate.com

## TREASURE TROVE

Long ago, pirates came in search of the treasure they thought was to be found here. They were looking for gold on this remote island, but their spades struck only rock. The real treasure was not buried, but clearly able to be seen, in the rich green landscape and hoard of birdlife. High on the cliffs, hidden amongst cashew and almond trees, is some more fortune: the villas of the resort Fregate Island Private. Each villa is set apart and blends into its lush background. The spectacular sea views, secluded beaches, and coral reef protected waters are just some of the spoils for those who are privileged to stay here. Privacy is one more of the riches here. Giant tortoises might cross your path in this elite hideaway, but you will see few people. Even fewer sightings will be made of the world's rarest bird,

the magpie robin. But you may hear its song, one thought so beautiful that the bird was sought for a life of captivity in gilded cages. Now it has found refuge on one of the most unspoiled places on earth. A safe haven that it shares, with others who seek to turn their backs on the outside world for a while.
◆ Book to pack: "Treasure Island" by Robert Louis Stevenson.

**DIRECTIONS** *A 20-minute flight from the international airport at Mahé by a private chartered aircraft* · **RATES** *€€€€* · **ROOMS** *16 pool villas, 1 Banyan Hill Estate* · **FOOD** *International and local gourmet cuisine, many ingredients grown on the resort's organic farm* · **X-FACTOR** *Seclusion and luxury faraway in exotic surroundings*

# EINE SCHATZINSEL

Vor langer Zeit kamen Piraten hierher, um den Schatz zu heben, den sie hier vermuteten. Es war Gold, wonach sie auf dieser abgelegenen Insel suchten, doch ihre Spaten stießen nur auf Felsgestein. Der wahre Schatz der Insel lag nirgendwo vergraben, sondern deutlich sichtbar in der üppigen grünen Landschaft und dem Reichtum der Vogelwelt. Hoch oben auf den Klippen verbirgt sich eine weitere Kostbarkeit: die Villen des Resorts Fregate Island Private. Jede der Villen steht für sich allein und fügt sich harmonisch in den sattgrünen Hintergrund ein. Der Meeresblick, die Strände und die geschützten Korallenriffgewässer sind nur einige der Annehmlichkeiten, die sich jenen bieten, die das Glück haben, hier verweilen zu dürfen. Ein weiterer Reichtum der Insel ist die Ungestörtheit, die man hier genießt. Und während einem an diesem exklusiven Zufluchtsort durchaus einige Riesenschildkröten begegnen können, trifft man Menschen hier eher selten. Noch weniger oft wird es einem gelingen, einen Blick auf die Seychellen-Schamadrossel zu erhaschen, den seltensten Vogel der Welt. Doch man kann sie singen hören und ihr Gesang galt lange Zeit als so betörend schön, dass diese Vögel gejagt wurden, um ihr Leben in goldenen Käfigen gefangen zu fristen. Heute haben sie einen geschützten Zufluchtsort in einem der unberührtesten Flecken der Erde gefunden – ein sicherer Hafen, den sie mit anderen teilen, die sich danach sehnen, dem Rest der Welt für eine Weile den Rücken zuzukehren. ◆ Buchtipp: „Die Schatzinsel" von Robert Louis Stevenson.

**ANREISE** *20-minütiger Flug mit einer privaten Chartermaschine vom internationalen Flughafen in Mahé* · **PREIS** *€€€€* · **ZIMMER** *16 Poolvillen, 1 Banyan Hill Estate* · **KÜCHE** *Internationale und lokale Gourmetküche; viele Zutaten stammen aus eigenem Bioanbau* · **X-FAKTOR** *Abgeschiedenheit und Luxus, entfernt vom Rest der Welt in exotischer Umgebung*

# L'ÎLE AUX TRÉSORS

Il y a de cela bien longtemps, des pirates débarquèrent sur cette île isolée, pensant y trouver un trésor. À la recherche d'or, leurs pelles ne rencontrèrent que du roc. Le véritable trésor, un luxuriant paysage verdoyant et une multitude d'oiseaux, n'était pas enfoui mais exposé à la vue de tous. Le sommet des falaises recèle d'autres joyaux, tapis à l'ombre des anacardiers et des amandiers : les villas de Fregate Island Private. Chacune d'entre elles a un style unique et se fond dans un paysage exubérant. Les vues spectaculaires sur la mer, les plages retirées et les eaux protégées par des barrières de corail ne sont que quelques exemples des trésors découverts par ceux qui ont le privilège de séjourner dans ce lieu. L'intimité et la solitude font partie des grandes richesses de cette retraite fastueuse, où votre chemin croisera peut-être celui de tortues géantes, mais plus difficilement celui de l'oiseau le plus rare du monde, le merle dyal. Toutefois, vous aurez peut-être la chance d'entendre son chant, si merveilleux que cet oiseau fut longtemps chassé puis gardé en captivité dans une cage dorée. Il a aujourd'hui trouvé refuge dans l'un des endroits les mieux préservés de la Terre, un havre de paix qu'il partage avec ceux qui souhaitent pour un temps oublier le monde extérieur. ◆ À lire : « L'île au trésor » de Robert Louis Stevenson.

**ACCÈS** *À 20 min de l'aéroport international de Mahé en avion-charter privé* · **PRIX** *€€€€* · **CHAMBRES** *16 villas avec piscine, 1 Banyan Hill Estate* · **RESTAURATION** *Cuisine gastronomique et locale, de nombreux produits sont issus de l'agriculture biologique insulaire* · **LES « PLUS »** *Cadre exotique et luxueux, à l'écart du reste du monde*

# CONSTANCE
# TSARABANJINA

## TSARABANJINA, MADAGASCAR

# CONSTANCE TSARABANJINA

207 Hellville, Nosy Be, Tsarabanjina, Madagascar
Tel. +261 32 051 5229 · resa@tsarabanjina.com
www.tsarabanjina.com

## TAKE TIME OUT

If you are impatient to reach this private paradise, arrive by helicopter; otherwise, take the time to travel by boat across the Indian Ocean and step out onto the white soft as powder sand beach. Your first footprint marks the start of your island time, and the opportunity for a stress-free holiday, if you can put off thoughts of having to go home. Cosseted from the real world, free from telephones and television, in an idyllic location, guests must still conform to a dress code. It is a very simple one – just relax, go barefoot. Described as a Robinson Crusoe-style experience, albeit with the luxury add-ons poor Crusoe never had, this is the place for you and your Man or Woman Friday to take time out. Ensconced in your bungalow, surrounded on three sides by lush tropical plants and facing the beach, a feeling of relaxation will set in quickly. You can lie in a hammock – there is room for both of you – and contemplate the beautiful landscape, or dive underwater to glimpse the amazing coral and the creatures that dwell there. Small to huge sea creatures are to be seen here; from turtles laying their eggs in the sand or being cared for in the turtle nursery, to humpback whales passing by from August to November on their way to give birth. The setting itself is stunning, and it is said that the people here add to the happy spirit of this place. And as you leave, you will be reminded that you can have a brass plate with your name on it fixed to the bar, if you come back to stay twice more in the future. You will want to return. ◆ Book to pack: "The Aye-Aye and I" by Gerald Durrell.

**DIRECTIONS** *65 km/40 miles off the north-west coast of Madagascar. The boat transfer from Nosy Be takes 90 minutes ·* **RATES** *€€€€ ·* **ROOMS** *25 straw-roofed, rosewood bungalows; each sleeps 2 and has its own ocean-facing veranda ·* **FOOD** *The restaurant serves freshly caught fish and, on request, lobster on the beach under a star-studded sky – very romantic! ·* **HISTORY** *The resort opened in 2006 ·* **X-FACTOR** *The massages on a natural rock plateau*

## AUS DER ZEIT GEFALLEN

Wer es gar nicht abwarten kann, in dieses Paradies zu gelangen, reist per Hubschrauber an. Alle anderen schippern gemächlich über den Indischen Ozean und betreten vom Boot aus den puderfeinen Sandstrand. Auf der Insel gehen die Uhren anders. Eine einmalige Gelegenheit für einen stressfreien Urlaub – falls Sie den Gedanken an die Heimfahrt ausblenden können. Abgeschirmt gegen die Realität, ohne Telefon und Fernseher, gilt es, inmitten dieses Idylls nur einen Dresscode zu befolgen: einfach mal loslassen. Barfuß gehen. Einmal wie Robinson Crusoe leben, wenn auch mit allem Komfort, der dem Ärmsten ja verwehrt war. Gemeinsam mit Ihrem (oder Ihrer) Freitag in den Tag hineinleben. Ihr privater Bungalow ist auf drei Seiten von tropischer Pracht umgeben, die vierte ist reserviert für den Ozean und Sie. So geht Entspannung pur! Genießen Sie die herrliche Landschaft von der Hängematte aus, die Platz für zwei bietet, bestaunen Sie beim Tauchgang die traumhafte Unterwasserwelt rings um Korallenriffs. Erleben Sie kleine und große Meerestiere, von Schildkröten bei der Eiablage im Sand und bei der Nachwuchspflege bis zu Buckelwalen, die von August bis November auf dem Weg zu ihren Kinderstuben vorüberziehen. Nicht nur die einzigartige Lage, sondern auch die Menschen tragen nachhaltig zur beglückenden Atmosphäre der Anlage bei. Wenn Sie noch zweimal wiederkommen, können Sie an der Bar eine Messingplakette mit Ihrem Namen anbringen lassen – und das ist nicht der einzige Grund, warum Sie nur zu gern wiederkommen werden! ◆ Buchtipp: „Naturerlebnis Madagaskar" von Gerald Durrell.

**ANREISE** *Rund 65 km vor der Nordwestküste Madagaskars. Der Transfer per Boot von Nosy Be dauert 90 Min.* · **PREIS** *€€€€* · **ZIMMER** *25 strohgedeckte Rosenholzbungalows für je 2 Personen jeweils mit eigener Veranda am Meer* · **KÜCHE** *Das Restaurant serviert frisch gefangenen Fisch und auf Wunsch am Strand unter dem sternenübersäten Himmel Hummer – sehr romantisch!* · **GESCHICHTE** *Die Anlage wurde 2006 eröffnet* · **X-FAKTOR** *Massagen auf einem natürlichen Felsplateau*

## FAITES UNE PAUSE

Si vous êtes impatient d'arriver dans ce paradis privé, prenez l'hélicoptère ; sinon, prenez le temps de voguer sur l'océan Indien jusqu'à la plage de sable blanc, doux comme du talc. Votre première empreinte marquera le début de votre séjour sur l'île, des vacances sans stress, si vous mettez de côté l'idée qu'il faudra un jour repartir. Choyés loin des contingences du monde réel, libérés du téléphone et de la télévision, lovés dans un endroit idyllique, les hôtes devront toutefois se soumettre à un code vestimentaire (au demeurant très simple) – décontracté et pieds nus. Cet endroit, qui promet une expérience à la Robinson avec, toutefois, des prestations de luxe dont le pauvre Crusoé n'a jamais pu jouir, sera parfait pour une pause avec votre moitié. Confortablement installés dans votre bungalow entouré sur trois côtés par une abondante végétation tropicale, face à la plage, vous ne tarderez pas à être envahis par une sensation de détente. Vous pourrez paresser dans un hamac – assez grand pour vous deux – et contempler le paysage magnifique, ou plonger à la découverte des incroyables coraux et des créatures qu'ils abritent. Vous pourrez vous livrer à l'observation de la faune : les tortues qui viennent pondre dans le sable et certains petits soignés dans une nurserie, mais aussi des baleines à bosse qui passent au large d'août à novembre, en route vers leurs zones de reproduction. Le cadre est à couper le souffle, et le personnel alimente l'atmosphère bienheureuse qui y règne. Quand vous partirez, on vous rappellera qu'une plaque en cuivre gravée à votre nom sera fixée au bar si vous revenez encore deux fois. Et vous aurez envie de revenir. ◆ À lire : « Le aye-aye et moi » de Gerald Durrell.

**ACCÈS** *À 65 km au large de la côte nord-ouest de Madagascar. Le transfert depuis Nosy Be prend 90 min* · **PRIX** *€€€€* · **CHAMBRES** *25 bungalows en bois de rose avec toit de paille pour 2 personnes avec leur véranda face à l'océan* · **RESTAURATION** *Le restaurant sert des poissons fraîchement pêchés et, sur demande, du homard, sur la plage, sous un ciel parsemé d'étoiles – très romantique !* · **HISTOIRE** *L'établissement a ouvert ses portes en 2006* · **LES « PLUS »** *Une île sanctuaire, et les massages sur un plateau rocheux naturel*

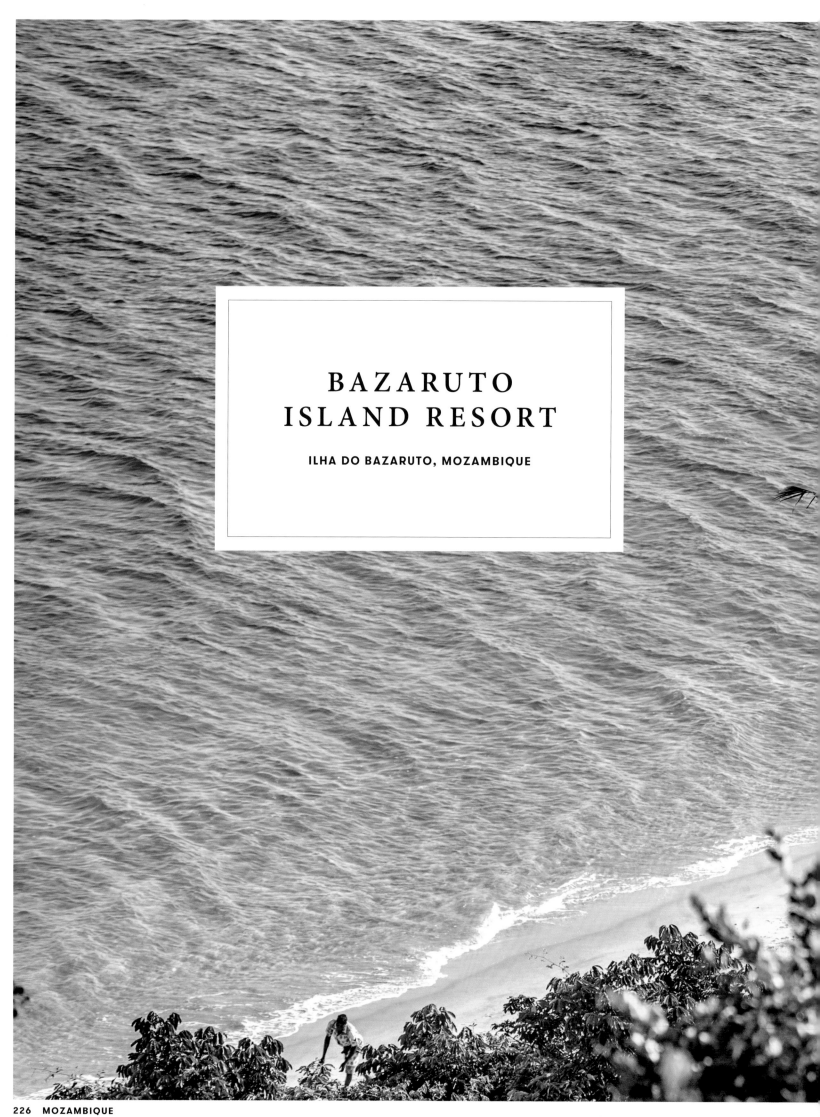

# BAZARUTO
# ISLAND RESORT

ILHA DO BAZARUTO, MOZAMBIQUE

# BAZARUTO ISLAND RESORT

Ilha do Bazaruto, Mozambique
Tel. +258 84 304 6670 and +27 10 003 8979 · bazaruto@anantara.com
www.anantara.com/en/bazaruto-island

## FAR AWAY

Bazaruto's greatest attraction is underwater: the Indian Ocean around the islands of this archipelago off the coast of Mozambique is a world of wonders. Countless tropical fish dart through the blue water, dolphins dance in the waves, and sea turtles glide past at a leisurely pace. Moreover, more than 100 kinds of coral grow in this nature reserve, which is also the habitat of East Africa's biggest population of the rare manatee, and each year between July and September these seas are visited by majestic humpback whales. Most divers and tourists explore the marine national park from a base in Vilankulo on the mainland, as the places accommodating guests on the islands themselves can be counted on the fingers of one hand. One of the few hotels in the archipelago is the Bazaruto Island Resort – in such a solitary, peaceful and idyllic spot that you feel you have discovered a different planet, a paradise. The villas right by the beach have been fitted out elegantly but without excessive luxury, using lots of wood. Thanks to floor-to-ceiling sliding doors, they open on to the ocean and feature outdoor extras such as open-air showers, hammocks and private pools.

The resort possesses a wonderful spa and three restaurants that serve fine fish dishes. Tartaruga, open to the skies, where guests dine in the evening by candlelight beneath the stars, has bags of atmosphere. But eating here can be even more natural and romantic – at a private dinner on a sandbank or on board a traditional dhow, sailing into the sunset. ◆ Book to pack: "Under the Frangipani" by Mia Couto.

DIRECTIONS *30 km/19 miles off the coast of Mozambique on the largest island of the archipelago. Transfer from Vilankulo takes 45 minutes by boat, 15 minutes by helicopter or propeller aircraft ·* RATES *€€€€; all-inclusive ·* ROOMS *44 villas for up to 4 persons, some with a private pool ·* FOOD *Fish and seafood, prepared according to recipes from Mozambique and Portugal, and with herbs from the resort's own garden ·* HISTORY *Bazaruto has been a nature reserve since 1971. The hotels of the archipelago cooperate with the WWF to ensure environmentally friendly tourism ·* X-FACTOR *Far from the world and very close to nature*

# WEIT WEG

Die größte Attraktion von Bazaruto liegt unter Wasser: Der Indische Ozean rund um die Inseln dieses Archipels vor der Küste Mosambiks birgt eine Wunderwelt. Abertausende tropischer Fische schwirren hier durchs Blau, Delfine tanzen in den Wellen, Meeresschildkröten gleiten gemächlich vorbei. In diesem Schutzgebiet wachsen zudem mehr als 100 Korallenarten, es ist der Lebensraum von Ostafrikas größter Population der seltenen Seekühe, und jedes Jahr zwischen Juli und September wird es zum Revier majestätischer Buckelwale. Die meisten Taucher und Touristen erkunden den marinen Nationalpark von Vilankulo auf dem Festland aus, denn auf den Inseln selbst lassen sich Unterkünfte für Gäste an einer Hand abzählen. Zu den wenigen Hotels des Archipels zählt das Bazaruto Island Resort – so einsam, friedlich und idyllisch gelegen, dass man sich wie auf einem anderen, paradiesischen Planeten fühlt. Die Villen direkt am Strand sind mit viel Holz elegant, aber nicht übertrieben luxuriös eingerichtet, öffnen sich dank raumhoher Schiebetüren zum Ozean und bieten draußen Extras wie Freiluftduschen, Hängematten oder private Pools. Ein wunderbares Spa gehört ebenso zum Haus wie drei Restaurants, die feinen Fisch servieren. Sehr stimmungsvoll ist das „Tartaruga" unter freiem Himmel, wo abends im Schein von Kerzen und Sternen gegessen wird. Aber sogar noch mehr Natur und Romantik sind möglich – bei einem privaten Dinner auf einer Sandbank oder an Bord eines traditionellen Dau, das in den Sonnenuntergang segelt. ◆ Buchtipp: „Unter dem Frangipanibaum" von Mia Couto.

**ANREISE** *30 km vor Mosambik auf der größten Insel des Archipels gelegen. Der Transfer von Vilankulo dauert mit dem Boot 45 Min., mit dem Helikopter oder Propellerflugzeug 15 Min.* · **PREIS** *€€€€; all-inclusive* · **ZIMMER** *44 Villen für bis zu 4 Personen. Teilweise mit Privatpool* · **KÜCHE** *Fisch und Meeresfrüchte, zubereitet nach Rezepten aus Mosambik und Portugal und mit Kräutern aus dem eigenen Garten verfeinert* · **GESCHICHTE** *Bazaruto steht seit 1971 unter Naturschutz. Die Hotels des Archipels kooperieren mit dem WWF für einen umweltfreundlichen Tourismus* · **X-FAKTOR** *Weit weg von der Welt und ganz nahe an der Natur*

# LOIN, TRÈS LOIN

La plus grande attraction de Bazaruto se trouve sous l'eau : l'océan Indien qui baigne les îles de cet archipel au large des côtes du Mozambique dissimule un univers merveilleux. Des milliers et des milliers de poissons tropicaux foisonnent dans les eaux bleues, les dauphins s'ébattent dans les vagues, les tortues de mer glissent tranquillement. Plus de 100 espèces de coraux poussent dans cette zone protégée qui abrite la plus grande population de dugongs, une espèce menacée, d'Afrique de l'Est, et qui accueille chaque année, entre juillet et septembre, de majestueuses baleines à bosse. La plupart des plongeurs et des touristes explorent le parc national marin depuis Vilankulo sur le continent, car sur les îles elles-mêmes, les hébergements se comptent sur les doigts de la main. L'un des rares hôtels de l'archipel est le Bazaruto Island Resort – si solitaire, si paisible et si bien situé qu'on se sent comme sur une autre planète paradisiaque. Les villas de la plage sont élégamment meublées avec beaucoup de bois, sans être exagérément luxueuses ; elles s'ouvrent sur l'océan grâce à des portes coulissantes à hauteur de plafond, et offrent des extras extérieurs sous forme de douches, de hamacs ou de piscines privées. Un magnifique spa fait partie de la maison ainsi que trois restaurants qui servent des plats de poisson raffinés. Le « Tartaruga » en plein air offre une ambiance très romantique, vous pouvez y dîner le soir à la lueur des bougies et des étoiles. Encore plus de nature et de romantisme sont toutefois possibles – en dînant à deux sur un banc de sable ou à bord d'un boutre traditionnel qui navigue au soleil couchant. ◆ À lire : « La véranda au frangipanier » de Mia Couto.

**ACCÈS** *Situé à 30 km du Mozambique sur la plus grande île de l'archipel. À 45 min de bateau de Vilankulo, à 15 min en hélicoptère ou en avion à hélice* · **PRIX** *€€€€; tout compris* · **CHAMBRES** *44 villas pouvant abriter jusqu'à 4 personnes. En partie avec piscine privée* · **RESTAURATION** *Poissons et fruits de mer, préparés d'après des recettes mozambicaines et portugaises et relevés avec les fines herbes du jardin* · **HISTOIRE** *Bazaruto est un site naturel protégé depuis 1971. Les hôtels de l'archipel coopèrent avec le WWF afin de développer l'écotourisme* · **LES « PLUS »** *Très loin du monde et tout près de la nature*

# SAUSAGE TREE
# CAMP

## LOWER ZAMBEZI NATIONAL PARK, ZAMBIA

# SAUSAGE TREE CAMP

Lower Zambezi National Park, Zambia
Tel. +27 76 586 1927 · reservations@sausagetreecamp.com
www.sausagetreecamp.com
*Open from April 1 to November 15 only*

## WILDERNESS PARADISE

There is such a thing as a sausage tree; meat eaters may be delighted to know this. Sadly, for fans of sausages, it is not a real source of these treats. It is linked just in name only, and so called because its seedpods look like huge salamis. On the banks of the Zambezi, under a large and shady specimen of this tree, a camp has been created. The large white tents of Sausage Tree Camp sit high along the riverbank. These are marquees for connoisseurs of canvas, and come with all the creature comforts. Spacious and cool, the tents are simple and stylish. Welcome breezes waft through. Mahogany and acacia trees join with the sausages to form a thick forest that surrounds the camp on three sides. The view is over the river and a field of reeds; channels dotted with water lilies and, at times, with heavier things like pods of hippos. In the distance blue-tinged mountains seem to float on the horizon. This remote and unspoiled park is Zambia's newest. Huge herds of buffalo, elephant, and hippo are found here, along with lion, leopard and cheetah. Elusive and prickly creatures such as porcupines and honey badgers are also seen. Over four hundred species of bird have been noted in the area; the cry of the widespread African fish eagle often cuts through the air. Perhaps it is a sign that the fishing is superb here – for tiger fish, bream and huge catfish. ◆ Book to pack: "North of South: an African Journey" by Shiva Naipaul.

**DIRECTIONS** *Access by light aircraft from Lusaka, Livingstone and Mfuwe to Jeki airstrip. From there it is a 30-minute trip by car and boat to the camp. From Lusaka a transfer by auto and boat is also possible (c. 5 hours)* · **RATES** €€€€ · **ROOMS** *7 luxury tents and 1 family tent with two baths and its own pool* · **FOOD** *African aromas* · **HISTORY** *Opened in August 1996* · **X-FACTOR** *River boating in a wilderness paradise*

## PARADIESISCHE WILDNIS

Es gibt tatsächlich einen sogenannten Würstchenbaum, Fleischesser werden dies mit Freude zur Kenntnis nehmen. Traurig für alle Wurstliebhaber ist, dass an diesen Bäumen nicht wirklich solche Leckereien wachsen. Nur der Name verweist auf sie. Der Baum wird deswegen so genannt, weil seine Samenschoten aussehen wie riesige Salamis. Am Ufer des Sambesi, unter einem großen und Schatten spendenden Exemplar jener Art, hat man ein Camp errichtet. Entlang des Ufers liegen die weißen Zelte des Sausage Tree Camps – große Zelte für Kenner des feinen Segeltuches, die jeden erdenklichen Luxus bieten. Die geräumigen und kühlen Zelte sind einfach und stilvoll und ein angenehmer Lufthauch weht durch sie hindurch. Zusammen mit den Sausage Trees bilden Mahagoni- und Akazienbäume einen dichten Wald, der das Lager an drei Seiten umgibt. Der Ausblick geht auf den Fluss und ein Schilfrohrfeld hinaus; man blickt auf die Kanäle, die mit Wasserlilien und manchmal auch mit etwas schwereren Lebewesen, wie Nilpferdherden, übersät sind. Die in der Ferne gelegenen, bläulich gefärbten Berge scheinen am Horizont entlangzutreiben. Dieser abgeschiedene und unberührte Park ist der jüngste in Sambia. Hier trifft man auf große Büffel-, Elefanten- und Nilpferdherden, aber auch auf Löwen, Leoparden und Geparden. Auch publikumsscheue und kratzbürstige Lebewesen wie das Stachelschwein oder den Honigdachs kann man hier zu Gesicht bekommen. In der Gegend wird das Vorkommen von mehr als 400 verschiedenen Vogelarten verzeichnet, und oft durchschneidet der Schrei des weitverbreiteten afrikanischen Fischadlers die Luft. Dies ist womöglich ein Anzeichen dafür, wie hervorragend man hier Tigerfische, Brassen und Riesenkatzenwelse fischen kann. ◆ Buchtipp: „Der Regenkönig" von Saul Bellow.

ANREISE *Mit dem Kleinflugzeug von Lusaka, Livingstone und Mfuwe zum Flugplatz Jeki. Von dort gelangt man mit dem Auto und Boot in 30 Min. zum Camp. Von Lusaka aus ist auch ein Transfer mit Auto und Boot möglich (etwa 5 Std.)* · PREIS *€€€€* · ZIMMER *7 Luxuszelte und 1 Familienzelt mit 2 Bädern und Privatpool* · KÜCHE *Afrikanische Aromen* · GESCHICHTE *Eröffnet im August 1996* · X-FAKTOR *Flussschifffahrt in paradiesischer Wildnis*

## PARADIS SAUVAGE

Il existe bel et bien un arbre à saucisses. Voilà une nouvelle qui ravira les amateurs de charcuterie. Malheureusement pour eux, cet arbre ne produit pas réellement ces douceurs et n'a de saucisse que le nom, qu'il tire de ses cosses ressemblant à d'énormes salamis. C'est sur les rives du Zambèze, à l'ombre d'un très grand spécimen d'arbre à saucisses, que le Sausage Tree Camp a été construit. Les grandes tentes blanches installées le long du fleuve sont équipées de tout le confort matériel et enchanteront les connaisseurs. Spacieuses, fraîches, elles sont simples et élégantes, et une brise bienvenue y circule en permanence. Les acajous, les acacias et les arbres à saucisses forment une épaisse forêt qui borde le camp sur trois côtés. Le côté ouvert donne sur le fleuve, sur un champ de roseaux et sur des canaux parsemés de nénuphars qui accueillent parfois des invités de poids, les hippopotames. Au loin, les montagnes teintées d'azur semblent flotter sur la ligne d'horizon. Ce parc reculé et bien préservé est le plus récent du pays. D'immenses troupeaux de buffles, d'éléphants et d'hippopotames, des lions, des léopards et des guépards ou encore des créatures insaisissables et armées de piquants telles que le porc-épic et le ratel y cohabitent. Plus de 400 espèces d'oiseaux ont été répertoriées sur ce territoire, et le cri du pygargue vocifère, un aigle pêcheur très courant en Afrique, fend l'air à intervalles réguliers. C'est peut-être le signe que la pêche est de premier choix. Vous trouverez ici des poissons tigres, des brèmes et d'énormes poissons-chats. ◆ À lire : « Au nord du Sud : un voyage africain » de Shiva Naipaul.

ACCÈS *En avionnette depuis Lusaka, Livingstone ou Mfuwe jusqu'à la piste de Jeki. De là, prévoir 30 min en voiture et en bateau jusqu'au camp. Transfert depuis Lusaka aussi en voiture et en bateau (environ 5 h)* · PRIX *€€€€* · CHAMBRES *7 tentes de luxe et une tente familiale avec deux salles de bains et une piscine privée* · RESTAURATION *Cuisine de qualité mariant les saveurs africaines* · HISTOIRE *Ouvert en août 1996* · LES « PLUS » *Navigation sur le fleuve au cœur d'un paradis sauvage*

# SANDIBE
# OKAVANGO
# SAFARI LODGE

**OKAVANGO DELTA, BOTSWANA**

# SANDIBE OKAVANGO SAFARI LODGE

Adjacent to Moremi Wildlife Reserve, Okavango Delta, Botswana
Tel. +27 11 809 43 00 · contactus@andbeyond.com
www.andbeyond.com

## STUDYING THE TRACKS

You never know when you might need a few basic skills. Here at Sandibe Lodge, you can apply yourself to gaining some. Interpretive bush walks are in the care of a local San – Bushman – guide. This is your chance to learn traditional bush skills; like making rope from grasses, how to construct traps, light fires with friction sticks, and how to track animals. Or you can just sit and watch them. Elephants have walked the meandering paths by the camp for hundreds of years. Perhaps moved by this, the lodge has been built with a commitment to "treading lightly on the earth." No trees were felled in its construction; instead, the cottages were built in a natural clearing. Their roofs are thatched, but that is where the resemblance to a usual cottage ends. These are far removed from the sort that this English word often means. Their airy rooms are styled with a rich fusion of color and texture, and of tactile fabrics like silk and leather, woven mats, copper and rough-hewn wood. An exotic landscape surrounds them, a forest of wild palms and twisting trees, flanked by channels of a delta that contains 95 per cent of all the surface water in Botswana. The mud spires of giant termite mounds and great baobab trees stand out in the scenery. Sandibe is set in a backwater, and all the better for it. A wealth of wildlife, birds, and plants thrive in the grass-swept floodplains of the Okavango Delta. "The art of moving gently, without suddenness, is the first to be studied by the hunter, and more so by the hunter with the camera." Karen Blixen ◆ Books to pack: "Among the Elephants" by Iain and Oria Douglas-Hamilton; "The White Bone" by Barbara Gowdy.

**DIRECTIONS** *Accessible only by scheduled flights from Johannesburg to Maun or Kasane, followed by a 30-minute flight from Maun, or a 1.5-hour flight from Kasane and a short drive to the camp* · **RATES** €€€€ · **ROOMS** *12 suites* · **FOOD** *Pan-African cuisine* · **HISTORY** *Opened in 1998* · **X-FACTOR** *Unique cottages in an idyllic environment and exceptional wildlife viewing*

# AUF SPURENSUCHE

Man kann nie wissen, wann man einmal ein paar grundlegende Fertigkeiten gebrauchen kann. Hier, in der Sandibe Lodge, können Sie bei Kulturwanderungen durch die Buschlandschaft unter der Führung eines einheimischen San, eines Buschmannes, einige davon erwerben. Dies ist Ihre Chance, die Fertigkeiten zu erlernen, die ein Buschmann traditionellerweise beherrscht, zum Beispiel ein Seil aus Gräsern zu flechten, Fallen zu bauen, Feuer durch das Aneinanderreiben zweier Stöckchen zu entflammen und die Fährten der Tiere zu lesen. Oder aber Sie bleiben einfach sitzen und beobachten die Tiere nur. Seit Hunderten von Jahren schon ziehen die Elefanten entlang der Pfade, die sich am Camp vorbeischlängeln. Vielleicht war dies der ausschlaggebende Grund, warum man sich beim Bau der Lodge dazu verpflichtet hat, sanft vorzugehen, es wurde kein Baum für ihre Errichtung gefällt. Stattdessen baute man die Hütten in eine natürliche Lichtung hinein. Ihre Dächer sind strohgedeckt, doch damit endet auch schon jedwede Ähnlichkeit mit einer gewöhnlichen Hütte. Die Hütten, von denen hier die Rede ist, sind weit entfernt von dem, was dieses Wort im Deutschen oft impliziert. Eine luxuriöse Verbindung von Farben und Materialien verleiht den luftigen Räumen Stil: sinnliche Stoffe wie Seide und Leder, gewebte Matten und Kupfer kombiniert mit grob behauenem Holz. Umgeben sind die Hütten von einer exotischen Landschaft, einem Wald aus wilden Palmen und gekrümmten Bäumen, an dem die Kanäle eines Flussdeltas vorbeilaufen, das 95 Prozent des gesamten Oberflächenwassers in Botswana enthält. Gegen den Horizont zeichnen sich die Spitzen der riesigen Termitenhügel und beeindruckende Affenbrotbäume ab. Ein großer Vorteil von Sandibe ist, dass es in einem Stauwasserbereich gelegen ist. Im Gras- und Schwemmland des Okavango-Deltas tummelt sich eine reiche Artenvielfalt von Tieren, Vögeln und Pflanzen. ◆ Buchtipps: „Unter Elefanten" von Iain und Oria Douglas-Hamilton; „Der weiße Knochen" von Barbara Gowdy.

**ANREISE** *Nur per Linienflug von Johannesburg nach Maun oder Kasane mit anschließendem 30-minütigem Flug von Maun oder 1,5-stündigem Flug von Kasane und kurzer Autofahrt zum Camp erreichbar ·* **PREIS** *€€€€ ·* **ZIMMER** *12 Suiten ·* **KÜCHE** *Panafrikanisch ·* **GESCHICHTE** *Eröffnet im Jahre 1998 ·* **X-FAKTOR** *Einzigartige Hütten in idyllischer Umgebung und außergewöhnliche Einblicke in Flora und Fauna*

# REPÉRER LES EMPREINTES

Qui sait si certaines techniques de survie ne vous seront pas un jour utiles ? Pour en apprendre quelques-unes, venez à Sandibe Lodge. Un guide local San, un bushman, vous y attend pour vous entraîner dans des excursions commentées à travers la brousse. Vous aurez la possibilité d'apprendre les techniques traditionnelles, notamment comment élaborer une corde avec de l'herbe, construire des pièges, faire démarrer un feu à l'aide de morceaux de bois et suivre la trace des animaux. Vous pourrez également vous contenter d'observer le guide. Les éléphants qui arpentent les chemins sinueux du camp depuis des centaines d'années sont peut-être à l'origine de l'engagement des constructeurs de l'hôtel, « fouler la terre d'un pas léger ». Aucun arbre n'a été abattu pour la construction de l'établissement et les chaumières ont été érigées dans une clairière naturelle. Leurs toits sont recouverts de chaume, mais la ressemblance avec des chaumières traditionnelles s'arrête là. Ces chaumières-là n'ont pratiquement rien à voir avec la définition habituelle du mot : les chambres, claires et spacieuses, présentent une riche association de couleurs et de textures, des étoffes qui invitent à la caresse, par exemple la soie et le cuir, des tapis tissés, du cuivre et du bois équarri. Un environnement exotique entoure les pavillons : une forêt de palmiers sauvages et d'arbres volubiles bordée des canaux d'un delta qui contient 95 % de la totalité de l'eau de surface du Botswana. Les flèches de boue des monticules des termites géantes et les immenses baobabs tranchent sur le paysage. Sandibe est situé au cœur des eaux mortes, ce qui est tout à son avantage. Une profusion d'animaux sauvages, d'oiseaux et de plantes s'épanouit dans les plaines inondables du delta d'Okavango balayées par les herbes. ◆ À lire : « Les éléphants et nous » de Iain et Oria Douglas-Hamilton ; « Un lien sûr » de Barbara Gowdy.

**ACCÈS** *Seulement par vol régulier de Johannesburg à Maun ou à Kasane, puis 30 min d'avion depuis Maun ou 1 h 30 depuis Kasane, suivies d'un trajet de 10 min en voiture jusqu'au camp ·* **PRIX** *€€€€ ·* **CHAMBRES** *12 suites ·* **RESTAURATION** *Cuisine panafricaine ·* **HISTOIRE** *Ouvert en 1998 ·* **LES « PLUS »** *Des pavillons au style unique dans un cadre idyllique et une découverte exceptionnelle de la faune et de la flore*

# NXABEGA
# OKAVANGO
# TENTED CAMP

## OKAVANGO DELTA, BOTSWANA

# NXABEGA OKAVANGO TENTED CAMP

Moremi Wildlife Reserve, Okavango Delta, Botswana
Tel. +27 11 809 43 00 · contactus@andbeyond.com
www.andbeyond.com

## WATER WORLD

The money here is named after water, which seems a fitting choice in a country that is mostly dry. Its main unit is the "pula", which means rain, and it is split into "thebe" – raindrops. It is a gentle prompt that this is a land, and a continent, where water is precious. Water is not scarce in this part. Botswana is dry, but not here, in the Delta. "On safari" in this wilderness of clear water and tall grass, at dawn or at dusk, can be a truly buoyant event. A trip in a "mokoro" (dugout canoe), just gliding in slow motion through the maze of channels, is a memory to treasure. Papyrus reeds edge the waterways; silver flashes of fish break the surface; all sorts of creatures move in and across the grass; the air is warm and still. It will come back to mind when you are on a clogged motorway. In the language of the river bushmen, Nxabega means "place of the giraffe". The tents are on high legs too, raised wooden platforms. African ebony and strangler fig trees give shade to the camp; its style is one of subtle class, and from your veranda or the main lodge, the view is spectacular. There are few people here in this landscape, but it is full of wildlife. Birds are everywhere – in and on the water, in the reeds and the trees, on the ground and in the air. This is one of the few places in Africa where you can see the animals from the waterways; and they can see you. ◆ Book to pack: "Rain Fall" by Barry Eisler.

**DIRECTIONS** *Accessible only by scheduled flights from Johannesburg to Maun or Kasane, followed by a 30-minute flight from Maun, or a 1.5-hour flight from Kasane and a short drive to the camp* · **RATES** €€€€ · **ROOMS** *9 safari tents for up to 18 guests* · **FOOD** *A fusion of local ingredients with African flavours* · **HISTORY** *Opened in April 2000* · **X-FACTOR** *The Delta itself, one of the most extraordinary wild places in Botswana*

# WASSERWELT

Die Bezeichnung für Geld leitet sich hier von der Bezeichnung für Wasser ab. Eine treffende Wortverwandtschaft, wenn man bedenkt, dass dies ein überwiegend trockenes Land ist. Die größere Einheit der hiesigen Währung heißt „pula", was Regen bedeutet, und setzt sich aus den sogenannten „thebe", Regentropfen, zusammen – ein behutsamer Hinweis darauf, dass auf diesem Kontinent Wasser eine Kostbarkeit darstellt. In diesem Teil des Landes herrscht allerdings keine Wasserknappheit. Zwar ist Botswana sehr trocken, jedoch nicht hier im Delta. In der Morgen- oder Abenddämmerung kann man eine schwimmende Safaritour durch diese Wildnis aus klarem Wasser und hohem Gras machen. Eine solche Tour in einer „mokoro", einem Einbaumboot, bei der man langsam durch das Labyrinth von Kanälen gleitet, ist ein unvergessliches Erlebnis. Papyrus säumt die Wasserstraßen, silbern blitzen die Fische an der Wasseroberfläche, die verschiedensten Tiere bewegen sich im und über dem Gras, die Luft ist warm und ruhig. All diese Eindrücke werden plötzlich zu Ihnen zurückkommen, wenn Sie wieder einmal im Stau auf der Autobahn stehen. In der Sprache der Flussbuschmänner bedeutet Nxabega „Ort der Giraffe". Auch die Zelte haben hier lange Beine: Sie stehen auf hölzernen Plattformen. Afrikanisches Ebenholz und Würgefeigen spenden dem Camp, das in einem feinen, klassischen Stil gehalten ist, Schatten. Von der Veranda oder dem Hauptgebäude aus kann man eine spektakuläre Aussicht genießen. In dieser Gegend leben nur wenige Menschen, dafür umso mehr Tiere. Überall sind Vögel, in und auf dem Wasser, im Schilf und in den Bäumen, am Boden und in der Luft. Dieser Ort ist einer der wenigen in Afrika, an dem man die Tiere vom Wasser aus beobachten kann und sie uns. ◆ Buchtipp: „Regenroman" von Karen Duve.

ANREISE *Nur per Linienflug von Johannesburg nach Maun oder Kasane mit anschließendem 30-minütigem Flug von Maun oder 1,5-stündigem Flug von Kasane und kurzer Autofahrt zum Camp erreichbar* · PREIS *€€€€* · ZIMMER *9 Safarizelte für maximal 18 Gäste* · KÜCHE *Verschmelzung einheimischer Zutaten mit einer Auswahl afrikanischer Aromen* · GESCHICHTE *Im April 2000 eröffnet* · X-FAKTOR *Das Delta selbst! Es ist einer der außergewöhnlichsten Orte in der Wildnis Botswanas*

# ÉCLAT AQUATIQUE

L'eau est à l'origine du nom de la monnaie botswanaise, ce qui est tout à fait approprié pour un pays où, dans l'ensemble, le climat est sec. L'unité monétaire de référence du pays est le « pula », pluie, lui-même divisé en « thebe », gouttes de pluie. Ceci montre à quel point l'eau est un bien précieux dans le pays et sur le continent. Contrairement à ce qui se passe dans le reste du pays, l'eau ne manque pas dans la région du delta. Partir en safari, à l'aube ou au crépuscule, dans cette vaste étendue sauvage couverte d'eau pure et de hautes herbes peut s'avérer une expérience extrêmement vivifiante. Vous chérirez longtemps le souvenir de votre excursion à bord d'un « mokoro » (pirogue) glissant au ralenti à travers un dédale de canaux : les papyrus bordant les voies navigables, l'éclair argenté des poissons rompant la surface de l'eau, les multiples créatures s'enfonçant dans l'herbe, l'air chaud et calme. Toutes ces images vous reviendront lorsque vous vous retrouverez coincé dans un embouteillage sur l'autoroute. Dans la langue des « bushmen du fleuve », Nxabega signifie « maison de la girafe ». Les tentes du camp sont elles aussi dressées sur de « hautes jambes », ces pilotis qui soutiennent des plates-formes en bois surélevées. Installé à l'ombre des ébéniers africains et des figuiers des Banyans, le camp est d'une élégance subtile et la vue depuis votre véranda ou le hall principal est spectaculaire. La solitude du lieu n'est troublée que par l'abondance de la faune : les oiseaux sont partout, dans et sur l'eau, au milieu des roseaux et perchés dans les arbres, sur le sol ou dans les airs. Le delta est l'une des rares régions africaines où vous pouvez apercevoir les oiseaux depuis les voies navigables et où eux aussi peuvent vous observer… ◆ À lire : « La ville du désert et de l'eau » de Jean-François Ménard ; « Déluge » de Karen Duve.

ACCÈS *Seulement par vol régulier de Johannesburg à Maun ou à Kasane, puis 30 min d'avion depuis Maun ou 1 h 30 depuis Kasane, suivies d'un trajet de 10 min en voiture jusqu'au camp* · PRIX *€€€€* · CHAMBRES *9 tentes accueillant 18 personnes maximum* · RESTAURATION *Grand choix et possibilité de savourer des plats aux saveurs africaines* · HISTOIRE *Ouvert en avril 2000* · LES « PLUS » *Le delta lui-même, l'un des sites les plus extraordinaires du Botswana*

# MOMBO CAMP

OKAVANGO DELTA, BOTSWANA

# MOMBO CAMP

Moremi Game Reserve, Okavango Delta, Botswana
Tel. +27 11 257 50 00 · enquiry@wilderness.co.za
www.wilderness-safaris.com

## PAVILIONS IN THE WILD

This is where the sound of cameras might just be louder than the noises of nature. On safari now, most of the wildlife is seen through a lens, rather than down the sights of a rifle. Just who or what is the hunter here is pleasantly confused. Mombo Camp is most famous for the number of predators on show – the animal kind that is. Close to the camp is the home territory of many prides of lions, cheetahs, leopards and African painted dogs. The game viewing here is so good that this is where many documentary filmmakers and photographers choose to lie in wait for their quarry. As well as the great variety and mass of wildlife, the game reserve where Mombo is situated is endowed with a matchless diversity of landscape. Marshes and floodplains, acacia bushveld, grassland and mopane forests provide a habitat that suits and shelters many creatures. The habitat on offer to humans is under canvas, in tents that are a far cry from the usual. These are more like luxury pavilions, each one raised off the ground by wooden decks, with great views across the Delta. The scene inside is also one to admire.

◆ Book to pack: "Dangerous Beauty: Life and Death in Africa; True Stories from a Safari Guide" by Mark C. Ross.

**DIRECTIONS** *Accessible only by scheduled flights from Johannesburg to Maun or Kasane, followed by a 30-minute flight from Maun, or a 1.5-hour flight from Kasane and a short drive to the camp ·* **RATES** *€€€€ ·* **ROOMS** *12, in two independent camps, Mombo with 9 rooms and Little Mombo with 3 ·* **FOOD** *Gourmet African and Western style ·* **HISTORY** *Constructed about 30 years ago and reopened following thorough rebuilding in January 2018 ·* **X-FACTOR** *Prolific wildlife observed from a luxurious setting*

# PAVILLONS IN DER WILDNIS

Hier ist das Klicken der Kameraauslöser teilweise lauter als die Geräusche der Natur selbst. Wer heute auf Safari geht, betrachtet die wilden Tiere eben eher durch die Linse einer Kamera als durch das Zielfernrohr eines Gewehres. Wer oder was der Jäger ist, scheint hier auf angenehme Weise vertauscht zu sein. Mombo Camp ist berühmt dafür, dass man eine Unmenge an wilden Raubtieren – und Raubtiere sind sie nun einmal – zu Gesicht bekommt. Nahe beim Camp liegt das Heimatgebiet von Löwen, Geparden, Leoparden und Afrikanischen Wildhunden. Die Gegend eignet sich so hervorragend zur Wildbeobachtung, dass viele Dokumentarfilmer und Fotografen hierherkommen, um sich auf die Lauer zu legen. Das Wildreservat, in welchem Mombo liegt, besticht jedoch nicht nur durch die großartige Vielfalt seiner Tierwelt, sondern ist auch mit einer beispiellos abwechslungsreichen Landschaft gesegnet. Marsch- und Schwemmland, Akazienwälder, Graslandschaften und Mopanewälder stellen für viele Tiere einen idealen Lebensraum dar. Der unmittelbare Lebensraum der menschlichen Besucher liegt unter Segeltuchplanen, in Zelten, die alles andere als gewöhnlich sind. Sie erinnern vielmehr an Luxuspavillons; jedes einzelne steht auf einem hölzernen Deck über dem Grund und bietet einen großartigen Ausblick über das Delta. Auch innen herrscht eine einzigartige Atmosphäre. ◆ Buchtipp: „Afrika. Das letzte Abenteuer. Die Geschichte eines Safariführers" von Mark C. Ross.

ANREISE *Nur per Linienflug von Johannesburg nach Maun oder Kasane mit anschließendem 30-minütigem Flug von Maun oder 1,5-stündigem Flug von Kasane und kurzer Autofahrt zum Camp erreichbar* · PREIS €€€€ · ZIMMER *12, in zwei voneinander unabhängigen Camps, 9 Zimmer in Mombo und 3 in Little Mombo* · KÜCHE *Afrikanische Feinkost und westlicher Stil* · GESCHICHTE *Vor rund 30 Jahren erbaut und im Januar 2018 nach komplettem Umbau neu eröffnet* · X-FAKTOR *Luxuriöse Ausstattung im Schoß von Mutter Natur*

# PAVILLONS SAUVAGES

Ici, seul le crépitement des appareils photo est susceptible de couvrir les bruits de la nature. De nos jours, lors d'un safari, la plupart des animaux sont observés à travers un objectif plutôt qu'à travers la lunette d'un fusil. Il est difficile en ces lieux de distinguer le chasseur du chassé, ce qui s'avère tout à fait plaisant. Mombo Camp est en partie célèbre pour son grand nombre de prédateurs. (Nous parlons bien sûr des animaux !) Nombreuses sont les troupes de lions, de guépards, de léopards et les meutes de chiens sauvages africains qui ont établi leur territoire à proximité du camp. L'endroit est tellement idéal pour l'observation des animaux que de nombreux réalisateurs de documentaires et photographes ont choisi ce site pour guetter leur proie. Outre sa faune extrêmement variée et abondante, la réserve naturelle qui accueille Mombo est dotée d'un paysage à la diversité incomparable. Les marécages et les plaines inondables, les steppes à acacia, les prairies et les forêts de mopani sont des habitats parfaitement adaptés aux multiples créatures qu'ils abritent. L'habitat proposé aux visiteurs est fait de toile, mais les tentes qui les accueilleront n'ont rien à voir avec les tentes habituelles. Comparables à des pavillons de luxe, montées sur pilotis et pontons en bois, elles donnent sur les superbes paysages du delta. Et l'intérieur est tout aussi beau. ◆ À lire : « Grands chasseurs sous la lune : les lions du Savuti » de Beverly Joubert et Dereck Joubert.

ACCÈS *Seulement par vol régulier de Johannesburg à Maun ou à Kasane, puis 30 min d'avion depuis Maun ou 1 h 30 depuis Kasane, suivies d'un trajet de 10 min en voiture jusqu'au camp* · PRIX €€€€ · CHAMBRES *12, situées dans deux camps séparés : Mombo 9 chambres et Little Mombo 3 chambres* · RESTAURATION *Cuisine gastronomique africaine et occidentale* · HISTOIRE *Ouvert il y a plus de 30 ans et rouvert en janvier 2018 après une reconstruction complète* · LES « PLUS » *Observation de la faune depuis un cadre luxueux*

# GARONGA
# SAFARI CAMP

LIMPOPO PROVINCE, SOUTH AFRICA

# GARONGA
# SAFARI CAMP

Hoedspruit 1380, Limpopo Province, South Africa
Tel. +27 87 806 20 80  ·  reservations@garonga.com
www.garonga.com

## SAFARI FOR THE SOUL

Everyone needs to take a safari for the soul, some "time out" to find inspiration and to restore lost vigor. The tent camp of Garonga, with its billowy ceilings of cream-colored canvas is just the place for such a mission. The floors and walls are sculpted from clay. In this place your senses too can be shaped and soothed. The camp is the perfect place to relax and reflect. To ease your stress, special treatments are at hand in a secluded "sala" in the bush. Taking a long soak in the deep bath that is nestled in the bush is one of the most memorable experiences. Being in the midst of such natural splendor is invigorating in itself. A night spent sleeping in a tree house out in the superb landscape that surrounds the camp is another way to relax. You can even cast off your clothes. A popular option is spending the night on the Sleep Out deck, located 20 minutes away from Garonga Lodge and connected only via two-way radio. In the middle of the wilderness you'll become one with nature. The camp looks out over a riverbed, one that an elephant herd is drawn to visit. Watching from the terrace or pool, you can be sure that elephants will come out from the bushes and feed just a few meters away from you. ◆ Book to pack: "West with the Night" by Beryl Markham.

DIRECTIONS *Daily scheduled flights from Johannesburg to Phalaborwa and Hoedspruit. Transfers are available from airport to the camp* ·
RATES *€€€€* · ROOMS *6 tent bungalows; 3 suites* · FOOD *Delicious African barbecue dishes, but vegetarians too are well catered for* ·
HISTORY *Garonga Safari Camp built in 1997, Little Garonga in 2007* ·
X-FACTOR *Taking a bush bath under the stars*

# SEELENSAFARI

Jeder sollte einmal auf Seelensafari gehen, einmal eine Art Auszeit nehmen, um neue Inspirationen zu erlangen und verloren gegangene Vitalität wieder aufzufrischen. Das Zeltcamp von Garonga mit seinen gewölbten Decken aus cremefarbenem Segeltuch ist genau das Richtige für solch ein Vorhaben. Boden und Wände sind aus Lehm geformt. Hier können auch die Sinne neu geformt und verwöhnt werden. Das Camp ist der ideale Ort zum Entspannen und Nachdenken. Wer Stress abbauen möchte, kann sich spezielle Entspannungsbehandlungen in einer abgelegenen „Sala" im Busch gönnen. Ein langes, erholsames Bad tief verborgen in der Wildnis ist wohl eine der einprägsamsten Erinnerungen, die Sie mitnehmen werden. Sich inmitten solcher Naturschönheit zu befinden, ist an sich schon wohltuend. Eine Nacht in einem Baumhaus in dieser fantastischen Landschaft zu verbringen, ist eine wunderbare Methode, um neue Kräfte zu schöpfen. Selbst Ihre Kleider können Sie hier abstreifen. Eine Nacht auf dem Sleep Out genannten Baumhaus,

20 Autominuten von der Garonga Lodge entfernt und mit dieser nur per Funkgerät verbunden, ist eine begehrte Option. Mitten in der Wildnis werden Sie hier eins mit der Natur. Das Camp öffnet sich zu einem Flussbett hin, das von Elefantenherden aufgesucht wird. Wenn Sie auf der Terrasse oder am Bassin stehen, können Sie so gut wie sicher sein, dass Elefanten aus dem Busch kommen und nur einige Meter von Ihnen entfernt auf Nahrungssuche gehen. ◆ Buchtipp: „Westwärts mit der Nacht. Mein Leben als Fliegerin in Afrika" von Beryl Markham.

**ANREISE** *Tägliche Linienflüge von Johannesburg nach Phalaborwa und Hoedspruit. Transfer vom Flughafen zum Camp möglich ·* **PREIS** *€€€€ ·* **ZIMMER** *6 Zeltbungalows und 3 Suiten ·* **KÜCHE** *Köstliche afrikanische Grillgerichte; doch auch für Vegetarier wird gut gesorgt! ·* **GESCHICHTE** *Garonga Safari Camp wurde 1997 erbaut, Little Garonga 2007 ·* **X-FAKTOR** *Ein Bad im Busch unter Sternenhimmel*

# UN SAFARI DE L'ÂME

Tout le monde a besoin de reprendre des forces, de faire une pause pour retrouver inspiration, énergie et vitalité. Pour cela, rien de tel qu'un safari. Le camp de Garonga, avec ses tentes au plafond en toile crème se gonflant et ondoyant sous le vent, est l'endroit le mieux adapté à une telle entreprise. Tout comme les sols et les murs sculptés dans l'argile, vos sens reprendront forme et s'apaiseront. Le camp est le lieu idéal pour se détendre et réfléchir : pour calmer votre stress, des soins spéciaux vous sont proposés dans un « sala » retiré situé en pleine brousse. Un long bain dans les vastes bassins à l'air libre est une expérience inoubliable, et la nature alentour est en elle-même revigorante. Vous pouvez également vous détendre en passant une nuit dans une cabane perchée dans un arbre, au milieu du superbe paysage qui entoure le camp. Vous pouvez même oublier vos vêtements. Une nuit passée dans la cabane perchée, à 20 minutes en voiture du Garonga Lodge et uniquement

joignable par radio, est une option très prisée. Au cœur de la nature, vous ne ferez plus qu'un avec elle. Le camp donne sur le lit d'un fleuve près duquel vous apercevrez peut-être un troupeau d'éléphants. Si vous observez le paysage depuis la terrasse ou la piscine, vous les verrez sortir des buissons et se nourrir à seulement quelques mètres de vous. ◆ À lire : « Vers l'ouest avec la nuit » de Beryl Markham.

**ACCÈS** *Vols quotidiens en partance de Johannesburg jusqu'à Phalaborwa et Hoedspruit. Possibilité de transfert de l'aéroport jusqu'au camp ·* **PRIX** *€€€€ ·* **CHAMBRES** *6 tentes-bungalows et 3 suites ·* **RESTAURATION** *Savoureuses grillades africaines, mais les végétariens ne sont pas oubliés ·* **HISTOIRE** *Le Safari Camp de Garonga a été construit en 1997, Little Garonga en 2007 ·* **LES « PLUS »** *Prendre un bain dans la brousse, sous les étoiles*

# SINGITA
# BOULDERS LODGE

## SABI SAND GAME RESERVE,
## NEAR KRUGER NATIONAL PARK, SOUTH AFRICA

# SINGITA
# BOULDERS LODGE

Sabi Sand Game Reserve, near Kruger National Park, Mpumalanga Province, South Africa
Tel. +27 21 68 33 424 · reservations@singita.com
www.singita.com

## WHERE THE BUFFALO ROAMS

In the heart of Africa, the search for prey is as old as time. As the sun starts to set and the heat of the day subsides, lions, leopards, cheetahs, hyenas and jackals begin to hunt. Whatever each of them outruns will be on their menu. Of course your dinner will be served to you; unlike the animals, you are not required to hunt down your food. At dusk, your personal game guard will escort you from your suite at the deluxe Boulders Lodge to the open-air "boma", for pre-dinner drinks around a blazing fire. Seated here, you can gaze out over the vast plains inside the exclusive wildlife sanctuary of Singita. For an animal lover Singita is a dream come true. The park has a wealth of wildlife. The top five on the animal kingdom list, the elephant, lion, leopard, buffalo and rhinoceros are all here. From your private deck at this sumptuous lodge, you can watch hippos feeding nearby and elephant drinking and spot a giraffe moving gracefully past. Whether traveling by day in vehicles, on walking expeditions to get close to the smaller inhabitants of the bush, or on night safaris to view rare nocturnal creatures, there is much to observe. ◆ Book to pack: "The Power of One" by Bryce Courtenay.

DIRECTIONS *A 1-hour flight north-east from Johannesburg to Singita airstrip, approximately 6.5 hours driving time from Johannesburg to Singita* · RATES *€€€€* · ROOMS *8 river suites, 2 bush suites, 1 family suite* · FOOD *African-inspired dishes – many delicious specialities from the barbecue!* · HISTORY *Opened in December 1996* · X-FACTOR *A luxury vantage point. A lot of leopards live in this area*

# IM KÖNIGREICH DER TIERE

Das Jagen nach Beute ist im Herzen Afrikas so alt wie die Zeit selbst. Wenn die Sonne allmählich untergeht und die Hitze des Tages abklingt, begeben sich Löwen, Leoparden, Geparden, Hyänen und Schakale auf die Jagd. Was auch immer sie sich erhetzen, steht auf ihrem Speiseplan. Im Gegensatz zu den Tieren müssen Sie nicht erst selbst auf die Jagd gehen. In der Abenddämmerung geleitet Sie Ihr persönlicher Wildwächter von Ihrer Suite in der luxuriösen Boulders Lodge zu der unter freiem Himmel gelegenen „boma", wo Sie, während Sie an einem lodernden Feuer sitzen, einen Aperitif einnehmen. Von hier kann man seinen Blick schweifen lassen über die weiten Ebenen, die innerhalb des Naturschutzparks von Singita liegen. Für Tierliebhaber ist Singita ein wahr gewordener Traum. Der Park beheimatet eine Fülle von wild lebenden Tieren. Die fünf wohl imposantesten Mitglieder im Königreich der Tiere, der Elefant, der Löwe, der Leopard, der Büffel und das Nashorn – sie alle leben hier. Von Ihrer privaten Terrasse aus können Sie in dieser feudalen Unterkunft Nilpferde beim Fressen und Elefanten beim Trinken beobachten oder eine Giraffe entdecken, die anmutigen Schrittes vorüberzieht. Ob auf Tagestouren mit dem Auto, bei Wanderexpeditionen, die einen näher an die kleineren Buschbewohner herankommen lassen, oder auf nächtlichen Safaris, bei denen man seltene Nachtwesen erspähen kann – es gibt viel zu beobachten. ◆ Buchtipp: „Der Glanz der Sonne" von Bryce Courtenay.

**ANREISE** *Nordöstlich von Johannesburg gelegen, 1-stündiger Flug von dort zum Singita-Airstrip, mit dem Auto etwa 6,5-stündige Fahrt von Johannesburg* · **PREIS** *€€€€* · **ZIMMER** *8 Flusssuiten, 2 Buschsuiten, 1 Familiensuite* · **KÜCHE** *Afrikanisch inspirierte Gerichte - viele köstliche Grillspezialitäten!* · **GESCHICHTE** *Eröffnet im Dezember 1996* · **X-FAKTOR** *Luxuriöser Aussichtspunkt. In der Gegend leben besonders viele Leoparden*

# AU ROYAUME DES ANIMAUX

En Afrique, la chasse remonte à la nuit des temps. Au crépuscule, lorsque la chaleur décroît, lions, léopards, guépards, hyènes et chacals commencent à traquer leur proie, et tout ce qui tombe sous leurs griffes figure à leur menu. Quant à vous, ne vous inquiétez pas. À la différence des animaux, vous n'aurez pas à chasser pour manger à votre faim. Au crépuscule, vous quitterez votre suite du luxueux Boulders Lodge escorté par votre garde-chasse personnel et rejoindrez le « boma » à l'air libre pour un apéritif autour d'un grand feu. Vous pourrez alors contempler les vastes plaines de l'exceptionnelle réserve d'animaux sauvages de Singita. Avec sa faune abondante, le parc de Singita est un rêve devenu réalité pour les amateurs d'animaux. Les cinq espèces les plus emblématiques du règne animal, à savoir l'éléphant, le lion, le léopard, le buffle et le rhinocéros, sont toutes représentées. Depuis votre terrasse privée vous pouvez observer des hippopotames en train de se nourrir et les éléphants s'abreuver, ou découvrir une girafe qui chemine gracieusement aux abords de l'hôtel. Que vous partiez de jour, en voiture ou à pied, à la découverte des autres animaux de la brousse ou que vous observiez des créatures nocturnes rares lors d'un safari de nuit, vous aurez beaucoup à voir. ◆ À lire : « La puissance de l'ange » de Bryce Courtenay.

**ACCÈS** *1 h de vol, direction nord-est, de Johannesburg jusqu'à la piste de Singita. En voiture, environ 6 h 30 de Johannesburg à Singita* · **PRIX** *€€€€* · **CHAMBRES** *8 suites donnant sur le fleuve, 2 suites sur la brousse, 1 suite familiale* · **RESTAURATION** *Plats inspirés des saveurs africaines, spécialités de grillades succulentes* · **HISTOIRE** *Ouvert en décembre 1996* · **LES « PLUS »** *Point de vue incomparable. De nombreux léopards vivent dans la région*

# ULUSABA

SABI SAND GAME RESERVE,
NEAR KRUGER NATIONAL PARK, SOUTH AFRICA

# ULUSABA

Sabi Sand Game Reserve, near Kruger National Park, P.O. Box 2220, Hazyview 1242, Mpumalanga Province, South Africa
Tel. +27 13 735 5460 (lodge) and +27 11 325 4405 (reservations) · enquiries@ulusaba.virgin.com
www.ulusaba.virgin.com

## DOUBLE CLASS

There are two equally appealing lodges to choose from here at Ulusaba. The Rock Lodge, perched castle-like on top of a granite hill, looks out across the bush to the distant Drakensberg Mountain range. Just 500 meters away, on the banks of a dry riverbed and under a canopy of trees, is the tree-house style Safari Lodge. Guests at either are fortunate to share much of the riches that are on offer. Both lodges, and the Ulusaba Private Game Reserve, are owned by Sir Richard Branson, and part of the Virgin Limited Edition collection of very special places to stay. As one might expect, there are some unique features here. Naturally, its central offer are the game drives that set out each morning and early evening in search of wildlife sightings. Lions, elephants and leopards are the undisputed superstars. When seen, they look on, or away, as cameras capture their likeness. Many smaller animals and birds make an appearance too. Between drives or safari walks, there are several options. You can choose to do very little other than lounging by or in the pool or relaxing in the spa. Or select an excursion to see spectacular canyons and waterfalls. You could learn how to whisper to elephants, and then ride one. If you decide to play tennis in the evening, the watchful eyes of a security escort will be on the lookout just in case any animals try to join in your game. At night, stargazing is irresistible and splendid. Guests can fine dine under the stars and then take a closer look at the celestial display above, through the telescope in the observatory that rises out of the bush. ◆ Book to pack: "Summertime" by J. M. Coetzee.

DIRECTIONS *Situated in the west of the Sabi Sand Game Reserve next to a private landing strip, 80 minutes flying time from Johannesburg ·* RATES €€€€ · ROOMS *20 rooms in Ulusaba, 8 in the Rock Lodge and 10 in the Safari Lodge ·* FOOD *Outstanding Pan-African cuisine ·* HISTORY *Ulusaba was purchased by Sir Richard Branson in 1994 and rock and safari lodges were rebuilt and added to ·* X-FACTOR *The lodge primarily employs locals and supports nearby villages with charity projects*

# KLASSE IM DOPPELPACK

In Ulusaba stehen gleich zwei attraktive Unterkünfte zur Wahl. Die Rock Lodge schmiegt sich wie eine Burg an die Spitze eines Granithügels und bietet einen weiten Blick über den Busch bis zu den Drakensbergen. Die nur 500 Meter entfernte Safari Lodge am Ufer eines trockenen Flussbetts wirkt unter dem Blätterdach auf den ersten Blick wie ein Baumhaus. So gut wie alle Annehmlichkeiten stehen den Gästen beider Häuser zur Verfügung. Die Lodges gehören ebenso wie das gesamte Ulusaba Private Game Reserve Sir Richard Branson und sind Teil der Virgin Limited Edition. Wie bei diesem Kaleidoskop einzigartiger Luxushotels zu erwarten, findet man auch hier das ganz Besondere. Eine zentrale Rolle spielen natürlich die Fotosafaris, bei denen man morgens und abends wilde Tiere aus nächster Nähe erlebt. Die unbestrittenen Superstars sind Löwen, Elefanten und Leoparden, die teils interessiert in die Kameralinse schauen, teils gelangweilt wegsehen, aber auch viele kleinere Tiere bekommt man zu Gesicht. Zwischen den Safarifahrten und -wanderungen bieten sich diverse Aktivitäten an. Wer mag, kann am Pool relaxen, im Spa chillen oder Ausflüge zu spektakulären Schluchten und Wasserfällen machen, Elefantenflüsterer bei der Arbeit erleben und auf einem der Riesen reiten. Bei der abendlichen Partie Tennis achten wachsame Security-Leute darauf, dass keine Tiere mitzuspielen versuchen. Die Nächte unter dem glitzernden Sternenzelt sind ein Erlebnis für sich, beim exzellenten Abendessen unter freiem Himmel ebenso wie beim anschließenden Blick durch das Teleskop des Observatoriums hoch über den Baumkronen. ◆ Buchtipp: „Sommer des Lebens" von J. M. Coetzee.

ANREISE *Westlich des Sabi Sand Game Reserve, in der Nähe eines privaten Start- und Landestreifens gelegen. Mit dem Flugzeug von Johannesburg in 80 Min. zu erreichen* · PREIS €€€€ · ZIMMER *20 Zimmer in Ulusaba, 8 in der Rock Lodge und 10 in der Safari Lodge* · KÜCHE *Vorzügliche panafrikanische Küche* · GESCHICHTE *Sir Richard Branson kaufte Ulusaba 1994 und ließ die Rock Lodge und Safari Lodge renovieren und erweitern* · X-FAKTOR *Die Lodge beschäftigt überwiegend Ortsansässige und unterstützt die umliegenden Dörfer durch gemeinnützige Projekte*

# DOUBLE CLASSE

Vous aurez le choix entre deux lodges aussi séduisants l'un que l'autre ici, à Ulusaba. Le Rock Lodge, perché comme un château d'antan au sommet d'une colline de granit, surplombe le bush jusqu'à la lointaine chaîne du Drakensberg. À seulement 500 mètres de là, sur les berges asséchées d'un lit de rivière et sous la canopée, vous trouverez le Safari Lodge et ses cabanes perchées dans les arbres. Les hôtes de l'un et de l'autre auront en partage les maintes richesses qui s'offrent à eux. Les deux lodges, tout comme l'ensemble de la Réserve privée d'Ulusaba, appartiennent à Sir Richard Branson, et font partie de la collection limitée des établissements hors du commun estampillés Virgin. Comme on peut s'y attendre, ils proposent des prestations uniques. L'attrait principal qu'ils ont en commun, ce sont bien sûr les expéditions organisées pour observer les animaux, tous les matins et en début de soirée. Lions, éléphants et léopards en sont les vedettes incontestées. Vous croiserez sans doute leur regard, ou ils le détourneront, vous laissant immortaliser leur majesté. Des animaux plus petits et de nombreux oiseaux se laissent aussi observer. Entre deux promenades à pied ou en voiture, les occupations ne manquent pas. Vous pourrez vous contenter de paresser à la piscine, de vous relaxer au spa, de choisir une excursion à la découverte de cascades et de canyons spectaculaires ou d'apprendre à chuchoter à l'oreille des éléphants, puis d'en monter un. Si vous optez pour une partie de tennis dans la soirée, un gardien vigilant au regard perçant vous accompagnera, au cas où un animal déciderait de venir jouer avec vous. La nuit, les étoiles offrent un spectacle irrésistible et splendide. Vous pourrez prendre un dîner de gourmet sous ce ciel magnifique, avant d'aller le regarder de plus près, grâce au télescope installé dans l'observatoire qui se dresse au cœur du bush. ◆ À lire : « L'été de la vie » de J. M. Coetzee.

ACCÈS *Dans la partie ouest de la Sabi Sand Game Reserve, près d'une piste d'atterrissage privée, à 80 min de vol de Johannesburg* · PRIX €€€€ · CHAMBRES *20 chambres à Ulusaba, 8 au Rock Lodge et 10 au Safari Lodge* · RESTAURATION *Une cuisine panafricaine remarquable* · HISTOIRE *Ulusaba a été racheté en 1994 par Sir Richard Branson, qui y a fait reconstruire les deux lodges* · LES « PLUS » *Les lodges emploient prioritairement des locaux et soutiennent les villages voisins avec des projets humanitaires*

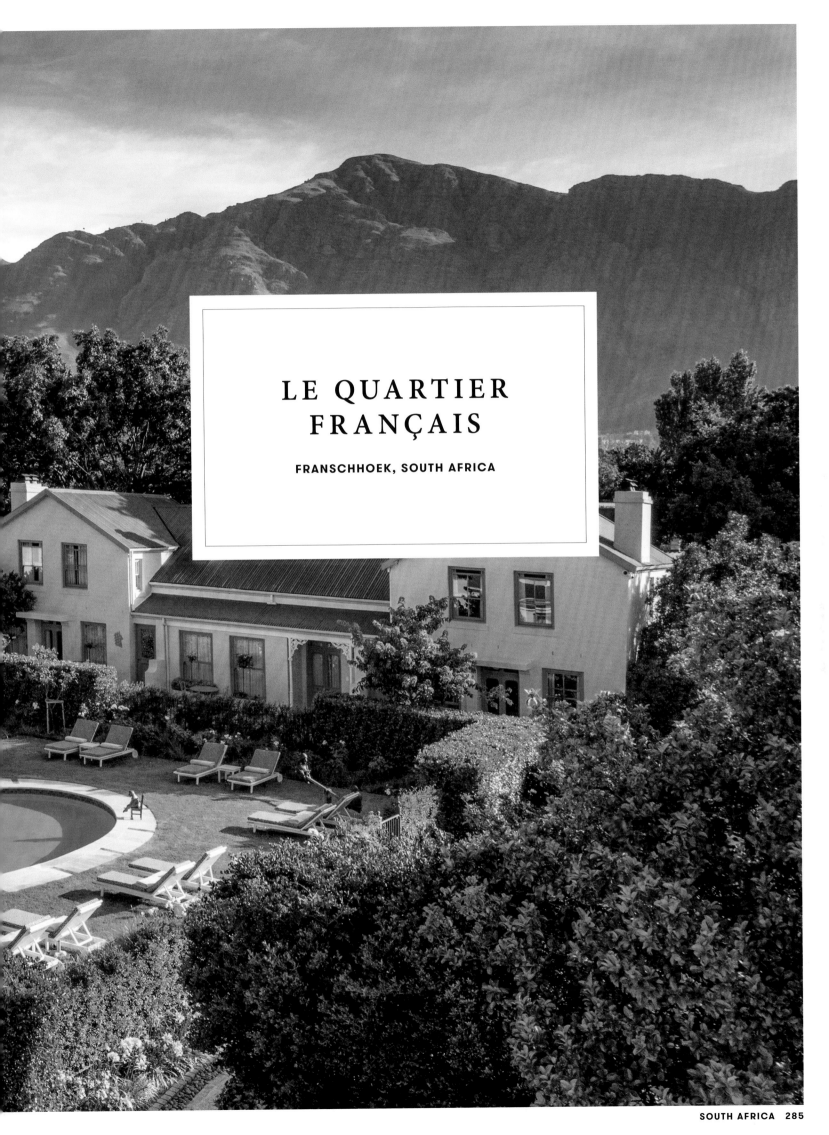

# LE QUARTIER FRANÇAIS

## FRANSCHHOEK, SOUTH AFRICA

# LE QUARTIER FRANÇAIS

Corner of Berg and Wilhelmina Street, 7690 Franschhoek, South Africa
Tel. +27 21 876 2151 (hotel) and +27 21 492 2222 (reservations) · reservations@leeucollection.com
www.leeucollection.com

## THE FRENCH SIDE OF SOUTH AFRICA

Franschhoek, the "French corner", dates back to the late 17th century, when Huguenots fled from France to the southern tip of Africa by sea after Louis XIV banned the Protestant religion on French soil and persecuted its adherents. Among the new arrivals at the Cape of Good Hope were wine farmers. They established the first vineyards in the region, which are among the best in the world today. Many farms, hotels and restaurants in Franschhoek have French names as reminders of this history – and one of them is Le Quartier Français. Beautifully situated in a garden with a pool, this boutique hotel accommodates guests in enchanting rooms and villas that the designer Beverly Boswell has furnished in a modern country-house style. The romantic elements here take their inspiration from France, while the large-format patterns and the more vivid colours are a link to South Africa. As Franschhoek is also a paradise for gourmets, this small hotel indulges itself in the luxury of two restaurants. Protégé, equipped with a show kitchen serves French, Italian and Asian-influenced dishes for sharing in a relaxed atmosphere. The focus in the gourmet restaurant Épice is on spices from all over the world, especially India – perhaps in homage to the founder of the exclusive group of hotels to which Le Quartier Français belongs today. He is a businessman with Indian roots who fell in love with South Africa and Franschhoek while on a trip to the football World Cup in 2010. Now he even engages in wine-making, and works with Chris and Andrea Mullineux to make excellent vintages from unusual and old kinds of grapes, such as Cinsault.
◆ Book to pack: "The Last Train to Zona Verde" by Paul Theroux.

DIRECTIONS *At the heart of Franschhoek, just under 1 hour's drive from the international airport at Cape Town ·* RATES *€€€€ ·* ROOMS *32 rooms in the hotel building and 2 villas (each with kitchen and pool) ·* FOOD *In addition to the hotel's two restaurants, the neighbouring Leeu Estates Hotel offers fine dining at La Petite Colombe and Le chêne (5 minutes' drive; there is a free shuttle service) ·* HISTORY *Opened in 1989, design makeover in 2017/18 ·* X-FACTOR *The spa at Leeu Estates, where extracts from South African Pinotage grapes are used in skin treatments*

# SÜDAFRIKAS FRANZÖSISCHE SEITE

Franschhoek, der „Franzosenwinkel", entstand im späten 17. Jahrhundert, als französische Hugenotten mit dem Schiff an die Südspitze Afrikas flohen, nachdem Ludwig XIV. den Protestantismus in Frankreich verboten hatte und die Gläubigen verfolgt wurden. Unter den Neuankömmlingen, die das Kap der Guten Hoffnung erreichten, waren auch Winzer – sie gründeten die ersten Güter in der Region, die heute zu den besten Weinbaugebieten der Welt gehört. Zahlreiche Höfe, Hotels und Restaurants in Franschhoek erinnern mit ihren französischen Namen an die Geschichte der Gegend – darunter auch Le Quartier Français. Wunderschön in einem Garten mit Pool gelegen, bietet das Boutiquehotel zauberhafte Zimmer und Villen, welche die Designerin Beverly Boswell im modernen Landhausstil eingerichtet hat. Die romantischen Elemente sind von Frankreich inspiriert; die großflächigen Muster und kräftigeren Farben stellen die Verbindung zu Südafrika her. Da Franschhoek auch ein Feinschmeckerparadies ist, leistet sich das kleine Haus den Luxus zweier Restaurants: Das Protégé mit seiner Showküche serviert in entspannter Atmosphäre französisch, italienisch und asiatisch angehauchte Gerichte zum Teilen. Das Gourmetrestaurant Épice spielt mit Gewürzen aus aller Welt, vor allem aus Indien – vielleicht eine Hommage an den Gründer der exklusiven Hotelgruppe, zu der das Haus heute gehört. Der Unternehmer mit indischen Wurzeln hat sich während der Fußballweltmeisterschaft 2010 in Südafrika und Franschhoek verliebt. Inzwischen ist er hier sogar selbst im Weinbau aktiv und lässt in Zusammenarbeit mit Chris und Andrea Mullineux hervorragende Weine aus außergewöhnlichen und alten Rebsorten wie Cinsault keltern. ◆ Buchtipp: „Ein letztes Mal in Afrika" von Paul Theroux.

**ANREISE** *Im Herzen von Franschhoek gelegen, eine knappe Fahrtstunde vom internationalen Flughafen Kapstadt entfernt* · **PREIS** €€€€ · **ZIMMER** *32 Zimmer, verteilt auf das Hotelgebäude sowie 2 Villen (jede mit Küche und Pool)* · **KÜCHE** *Neben den 2 hoteleigenen Restaurants gibt es im benachbarten Hotel Leeu Estates, das denselben Besitzer hat, die feinen Lokale La Petite Colombe und Le chêne (5 Fahrtminuten, ein kostenfreier Shuttle wird angeboten)* · **GESCHICHTE** *1989 eröffnet und 2017/18 neu designt* · **X-FAKTOR** *Das im Leeu Estates gelegene Spa, in dem die Haut mit Wirkstoffen aus der südafrikanischen Pinotage-Traube gepflegt wird*

# L'HÉRITAGE FRANÇAIS EN AFRIQUE DU SUD

Le Franschhoek, « le coin des Français », a vu le jour à la fin du XVIIe siècle, après la révocation de l'Édit de Nantes par Louis XIV, lorsque des huguenots français réfugiés en Hollande se sont établis dans la pointe sud de l'Afrique. Parmi les nouveaux venus qui ont atteint le Cap de Bonne-Espérance après une longue traversée, se trouvaient des viticulteurs qui ont fondé les premiers domaines dans la région, devenue l'une des meilleures régions viticoles du monde. Portant des noms français, de nombreux hôtels, restaurants et fermes de Franschhoek rappellent l'histoire des lieux – c'est le cas du Quartier français. Magnifiquement situé dans un jardin doté d'une piscine, le boutique-hôtel propose des chambres et des villas charmantes, que la designer Beverly Boswell a décorées dans un style campagnard moderne. Les éléments romantiques sont inspirés de la France ; les motifs à grande échelle et les couleurs plus vives font le lien avec l'Afrique du Sud. Comme Franschhoek est aussi un paradis pour les gourmets, la petite maison s'offre le luxe d'abriter deux restaurants : le Protégé, avec sa cuisine ouverte, sert des plats d'inspiration française, italienne et asiatique à partager dans une ambiance détendue. Le restaurant gastronomique Épice joue avec des épices du monde entier et surtout indiennes – peut-être en hommage au fondateur du groupe hôtelier exclusif auquel la maison appartient aujourd'hui. Celui-ci, un homme d'affaires aux racines indiennes, est tombé amoureux de l'Afrique du Sud et de Franschhoek en venant en 2010 assister à la Coupe du monde. Depuis, il s'occupe même activement de viticulture et, en collaboration avec Chris et Andrea Mullineux, fait fabriquer des vins exceptionnels à partir de cépages anciens comme le Cinsault. ◆ À lire : « The Last Train to Zona Verde : My Ultimate African Safari » (en anglais) de Paul Theroux.

**ACCÈS** *Au cœur de Franschhoek, à une petite heure de route de l'aéroport international du Cap* · **PRIX** €€€€ · **CHAMBRES** *32 chambres dans le bâtiment de l'hôtel ainsi que 2 villas (avec cuisine et piscine)* · **RESTAURATION** *En plus des 2 restaurants de l'hôtel, l'hôtel Leeu Estates voisin, qui a le même propriétaire, abrite les restaurants raffinés La Petite Colombe et Le chêne (à 5 minutes en voiture, une navette gratuite est prévue)* · **HISTOIRE** *Ouvert en 1989 ; le design a été revu en 2017/18* · **LES « PLUS »** *Le spa, également dans les Leeu Estates, où la peau découvre les bienfaits des principes actifs du cépage Pinotage cultivé en Afrique du Sud*

# BABYLONSTOREN

FRANSCHHOEK, SOUTH AFRICA

# BABYLONSTOREN

Klapmuts Simondium Road, 7670 Franschhoek, South Africa
Tel. +27 21 863 3852 · enquiries@babylonstoren.com and reservations@babylonstoren.com
www.babylonstoren.com

## IN THE GARDEN OF EDEN

Babylonstoren is one of the most impressive gardens in the Cape Town area. Laid out in exemplary manner by the architect Patrice Taravella and inspired by the Hanging Gardens of Babylon, by The Company's Garden in Cape Town, which once supplied fruit and vegetables to the ships of the Dutch East India Company on their stopovers at the Cape, and also by the classical French style of horticulture, Babylonstoren has more than 300 different varieties of plants, all of which are either edible or have healing properties. It is possible to visit the farm on a day trip from Cape Town – but it is much more pleasant to stay here for a few days. Karen Roos, formerly editor of "Elle Decor", has skillfully restored and extended the historic buildings at Babylonstoren. She has kept the traditional Cape Dutch style with thick whitewashed walls, curving gables and thatched roofs – but has combined this with modern glass cubes and designer furniture by Kartell, Magis, Philippe Starck and Ronan & Erwan Bouroullec. The outstanding main restaurant, Babel, occupies the old cow shed (whose former residents are now only present in the form of an outsized portrait of a cow), and Greenhouse, where all meals are served picnic-style, has the air of an idyllic hothouse for plants. The fruit, vegetables and herbs for both eateries come from the garden, of course. Guests are welcome to come along to the morning harvest and sample the produce. ◆ Book to pack: "The Covenant" by James A. Michener.

**DIRECTIONS** *East of Cape Town, 50 km/31 miles from the airport ·* **RATES** *€€€–€€€€ ·* **ROOMS** *9 suites in the farmhouse, 13 Garden Cottages (as suites or with 1 or 2 bedrooms), 6 Fynbos Cottages. The Manor House with 5 double rooms is available only for exclusive hire ·* **FOOD** *In addition to two restaurants there is The Bakery that serves Italian inspired dinners twice a week and hosts a five-course Carnivore evening on Wednesdays for the meat lover, as well as a wine tasting room ·* **HISTORY** *There was a farm here as long ago as the late 17th century, but it fell into decay. The present owners bought the farm in 2007 ·* **X-FACTOR** *The Garden Spa with a heated outdoor pool and vitality pool*

# IM GARTEN EDEN

Babylonstoren ist einer der beeindruckensten Gärten in der Nähe von Kapstadt. Das Gut ist mustergültig vom Architekten Patrice Taravella angelegt, der sich inspirieren ließ von den Hängenden Gärten von Babylon, vom Company's Garden in Kapstadt, der einst die Schiffe der Niederländischen Ostindien-Kompanie bei ihrem Zwischenstopp am Kap mit Obst und Gemüse versorgte, sowie von der klassischen französischen Gartenkunst. In Babylonstoren finden sich mehr als 300 verschiedene Pflanzenarten, die alle entweder essbar sind oder heilende Wirkung haben. Man kann das Gut bei einem Tagesausflug von Kapstadt aus besuchen – viel schöner ist es aber, gleich einige Tage lang hier zu wohnen. Karen Roos, früher Redakteurin bei „Elle Decor", hat die historischen Häuser der Farm gekonnt restauriert und erweitert. Sie behielt den traditionellen kapholländischen Stil mit dicken, weiß getünchten Mauern, geschwungenen Giebeln und strohgedeckten Dächern bei – kombinierte ihn aber mit modernen Glaskuben und Designermöbeln von Kartell, Magis, Philippe Starck oder Ronan & Erwan Bouroullec. Das hervorragende Hauptrestaurant Babel entstand im ehemaligen Kuhstall (die einstigen Bewohner sind nur noch auf einem überdimensionalen Kuhporträt präsent), und das Greenhouse, das alle Speisen im Picknickstil serviert, erinnert an ein idyllisches Gewächshaus. Obst, Gemüse und Kräuter für beide Lokale stammen natürlich aus dem eigenen Garten – Gäste dürfen bei der morgendlichen Ernte gerne dabei sein und schon mal vorkosten. ◆ Buchtipp: „Verheißene Erde" von James A. Michener.

**ANREISE** *Östlich von Kapstadt gelegen, 50 km vom Flughafen entfernt ·* **PREIS** *€€€–€€€€ ·* **ZIMMER** *9 Suiten im Farmhouse, 13 Garden Cottages (als Suiten oder mit 1 oder 2 Schlafzimmern), 6 Fynbos Cottages. Das Manor House mit 5 Doppelzimmern kann nur exklusiv gemietet werden ·* **KÜCHE** *Neben zwei Restaurants gibt es die Bakery, die abends zweimal in der Woche italienisch inspirierte Gerichte und mittwochs ein Fünf-Gänge-Menü für Fleischliebhaber serviert, sowie einen Weinkeller ·* **GESCHICHTE** *Bereits Ende des 17. Jahrhunderts gab es hier eine Farm, die später jedoch verfiel. Die heutigen Besitzer haben die Farm 2007 erworben ·* **X-FAKTOR** *Das Garden Spa mit beheiztem Außenpool und Vitality Pool*

# LE JARDIN D'ÉDEN

Babylonstoren est l'un des jardins les plus impressionnants près du Cap. Conçu par l'architecte Patrice Taravella qui s'est inspiré des jardins suspendus de Babylone, du « Company's Garden » au Cap, le jardin qui approvisionnait autrefois les navires de la Compagnie hollandaise des Indes orientales en fruits et légumes pendant leur escale au Cap, et de l'art paysager français classique, Babylonstoren abrite plus de 300 espèces végétales différentes, toutes comestibles ou possédant des propriétés curatives. Vous pouvez visiter la ferme pendant une excursion d'une journée depuis Le Cap – mais c'est beaucoup plus agréable d'y vivre quelques jours. L'ancienne éditrice de « Elle Decor » Karen Roos a habilement restauré et agrandi les bâtiments historiques de la ferme. Elle a gardé le style traditionnel de Cape Dutch avec des murs épais blanchis à la chaux, des pignons courbes et des toits de chaume – mais l'a combiné avec des cubes de verre modernes et des meubles design de Kartell, Magis, Philippe Starck ou Ronan & Erwan Bouroullec. Le restaurant principal Babel a vu le jour dans l'ancienne étable (les anciens résidents ne sont présents que sur un portrait de vache surdimensionné), et la Greenhouse, qui sert tous les repas en style pique-nique, fait songer à une serre idyllique. Bien sûr, les fruits, les légumes et les fines herbes préparés dans les deux restaurants proviennent de leurs propres jardins – les clients sont invités à se joindre aux cueilleurs le matin et à les déguster à l'avance. ◆ À lire : « L'Alliance » de James A. Michener.

**ACCÈS** *Situé à l'est du Cap, à 50 km de l'aéroport ·* **PRIX** *€€€–€€€€ ·* **CHAMBRES** *9 suites dans la ferme, 13 Garden Cottages (suites ou avec 1 ou 2 chambres à coucher), 6 Fynbos Cottages. La Manor House qui abrite 5 chambres doubles ne peut être louée qu'en exclusivité ·* **RESTAURATION** *À côté des deux restaurants, on trouve le Bakery qui propose deux fois par semaine des dîners d'inspiration italienne et le mercredi un dîner « carnivore » en cinq services pour les amateurs de viande ainsi qu'une pièce pour la dégustation du vin ·* **HISTOIRE** *Une ferme existait déjà ici à la fin du XVIIe siècle, elle est tombée en ruine plus tard. Les propriétaires actuels ont acheté la ferme en 2007 ·* **LES « PLUS »** *Le Garden Spa avec piscine extérieure chauffée et bain vitalité*

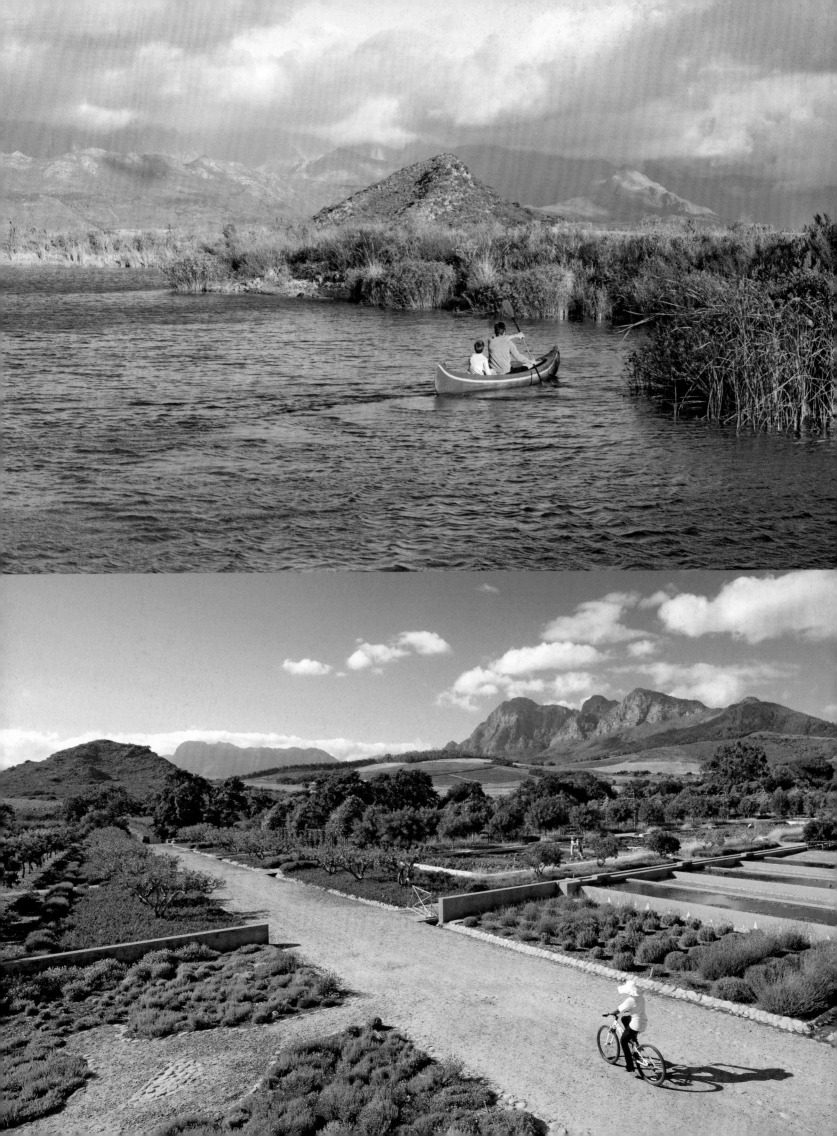

We press sun ripe grapes white & red
Chardonnay, Viognier, Chenin Blanc, Merlot, Semillon
Malbec, Mourvèdre, Cabernet sauvignon, Carbernet Franc
Shiraz, Petit verdot, Pinot noir, Pinotage

Flowers

We are harvesting

Fruits

Leaves  Spekboom, sweet potatoes & purslane
wild Italian Rocket, sorrel, olivia cos lettuce
various if mesclyn d, Basil- sweet, red, minette,
rigance, Thai, on Greek, Marjoram, tulsi.

Roots  Beetroot,                                              Seeds

                                          Atomic Red

                                                              Herbs
Stems

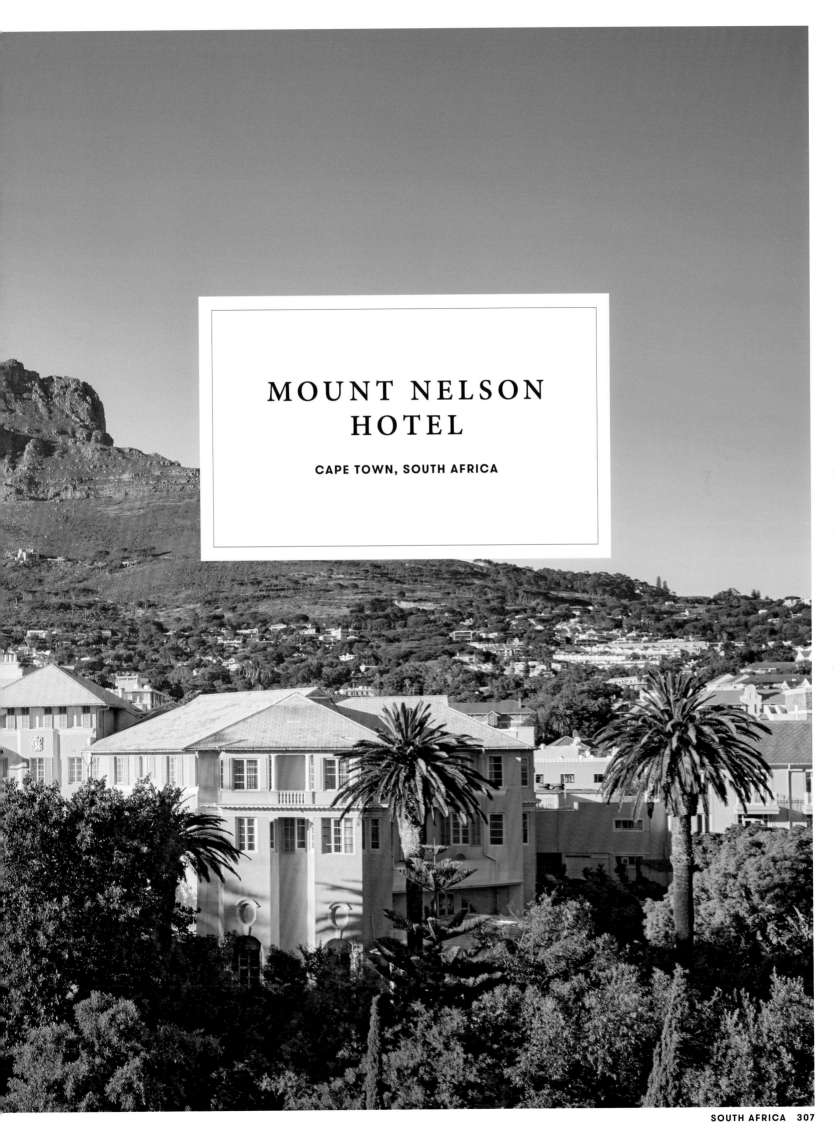

# MOUNT NELSON HOTEL

**CAPE TOWN, SOUTH AFRICA**

# MOUNT NELSON HOTEL

76 Orange Street, Gardens, 8001 Cape Town, South Africa
Tel. +27 21 483 1000 · reservations.mnh@belmond.com
www.belmond.com/mountnelsonhotel

## CLASSICALLY CAPE TOWN

The grande dame among Cape Town's luxury hotels has also been known as the "Pink Lady" ever since November 1918, when its director had it painted in that color to celebrate the end of the First World War. Opened in 1899 by the owner of the British Union Castle Shipping Line for the company's first-class passengers (the lovely curved wooden chairs in the restaurant once stood on the decks of ocean liners), the Mount Nelson Hotel has always welcomed the famous and powerful. Winston Churchill stayed here when he was a young correspondent, John Lennon reserved a room under his pseudonym "Mr. Greenwood" and meditated on the Table Mountain, and the Dalai Lama addressed 500 of his adherents, all sitting on the floor of the ballroom with crossed legs. You can sense the atmosphere that gave rise to these and many other anecdotes in the elegantly and exquisitely designed rooms. The suites in the Victorian cottages, fitted with four-poster beds, Venetian mirrors and open fireplaces, have views of the rose garden and are particularly luxurious. The aura of history is also perceptible in the Lord Nelson restaurant with its oak paneling, huge chandeliers and ornamented ceiling; and afternoon tea with delightful sandwiches and scones is also an established part of the tradition. The exotic garden around the hotel has an area of more than three and a half hectares – it is one of the city's most enchanting oases. ◆ Book to pack: "Ladysmith" by Giles Foden.

DIRECTIONS *At the foot of the Table Mountain, 20 km/13 miles from Cape Town airport* · RATES *€€€–€€€€* · ROOMS *198 rooms and suites* · FOOD *The restaurant serves avant-garde menus and offers seats at a chef's table. The bistro provides breakfast and service at the two pools* · HISTORY *Opened on 6 March 1899 – then the first hotel in South Africa with hot and cold running water* · X-FACTOR *The spa in three carefully restored Victorian buildings*

## KAPSTADT, GANZ KLASSISCH

Die Grande Dame unter den Luxushotels von Kapstadt wird auch „Pink Lady" genannt, seit sie der damalige Direktor im November 1918 rosa streichen ließ, um das Ende des Ersten Weltkrieges zu feiern. Vom Besitzer der britischen Union Castle Shipping Line 1899 für seine Schiffspassagiere der ersten Klasse eröffnet (die schön geschwungenen Holzstühle im Restaurant standen damals auf den Decks seiner Ozeandampfer), heißt das Mount Nelson Hotel alle willkommen, die Rang und Namen haben. Winston Churchill übernachtete hier als junger Korrespondent, John Lennon reservierte unter seinem Pseudonym „Mr. Greenwood" und meditierte auf dem Tafelberg, und der Dalai Lama sprach zu 500 seiner Anhänger, die alle mit gekreuzten Beinen auf dem Boden des Ballsaals saßen. Solchen und vielen weiteren Anekdoten kann man in den elegant und exquisit gestalteten Zimmer nachspüren – besonders luxuriös sind die Suiten in den viktorianischen Cottages, die mit Himmelbetten, venezianischen Spiegeln sowie offenen Kaminen ausgestattet sind und in den duftenden Rosengarten blicken. Viel Geschichte atmet auch das Restaurant Lord Nelson mit Eichenholzvertäfelungen, riesigem Kronleuchter und Deckenornamenten; und der Afternoon Tea mit erlesenen Sandwiches und Scones gehört ebenfalls fest zur Tradition. Umgeben wird das Hotel von einem exotischen Garten, der sich über dreieinhalb Hektar erstreckt – eine der bezauberndsten Oasen der Stadt. ◆ Buchtipp: „Die letzte Stadt von Afrika" von Giles Foden.

ANREISE *Am Fuß des Tafelbergs gelegen, 20 km vom Flughafen Kapstadt entfernt* · PREIS *€€€–€€€€* · ZIMMER *198 Zimmer und Suiten* · KÜCHE *Das Restaurant serviert Avantgarde-Menüs und bietet einen Chef's Table. Das Bistro sorgt fürs Frühstück und bedient an den zwei Pools* · GESCHICHTE *Am 6. März 1899 eröffnet – Südafrikas erstes Hotel mit fließend kaltem und warmen Wasser* · X-FAKTOR *Das Spa in drei sorgsam restaurierten viktorianischen Häusern*

## LE CAP, CLASSIQUE

La grande dame des hôtels de luxe du Cap est également connue sous le nom de « Pink Lady » – en novembre 1918, le directeur l'avait fait peindre en rose pour célébrer la fin de la Première Guerre mondiale, et ce nom lui est resté. Ouvert en 1899 par le propriétaire de la British Union Castle Shipping Line pour ses passagers de première classe (les belles chaises en bois cintré du restaurant se trouvaient à l'époque sur les ponts de ses paquebots), l'hôtel Mount Nelson accueille tous ceux qui se distinguent d'une manière ou d'une autre. Winston Churchill y a séjourné lorsqu'il était un jeune correspondant de guerre, John Lennon réservait sous son pseudonyme « M. Greenwood » et méditait sur la Montagne de la Table, et le Dalaï Lama parla à 500 de ses disciples, tous assis jambes croisées sur le sol de la salle de bal. Ces anecdotes, et bien d'autres encore, ressurgissent à l'esprit dans les chambres au design élégant et raffiné – les suites des cottages victoriens qui abritent des lits à baldaquin, des miroirs vénitiens et des cheminées ouvertes et donnent sur la roseraie parfumée sont particulièrement luxueuses. Le restaurant Lord Nelson avec ses lambris de chêne, son lustre gigantesque et son plafond ornementé est lui aussi chargé d'histoire ; et le thé de cinq heures qui propose des sandwiches et des scones exquis est ancré dans la tradition. L'hôtel est entouré d'un jardin exotique de trois hectares et demi qui est l'une des oasis les plus ravissantes de la ville. ◆ À lire : « Ladysmith » de Giles Foden.

ACCÈS *Situé au pied de la Montagne de la Table, à 20 km de l'aéroport du Cap* · PRIX *€€€–€€€€* · CHAMBRES *198 chambres et suites* · RESTAURATION *Le restaurant sert une cuisine d'avant-garde et propose un Chef's Table. Le bistro veille sur le petit déjeuner et sert les clients au bord des deux piscines* · HISTOIRE *L'hôtel a ouvert ses portes le 6 mars 1899 – il était alors le premier en Afrique du Sud à avoir l'eau courante froide et chaude* · LES « PLUS » *Le spa aménagé dans trois maisons victoriennes soigneusement restaurées*

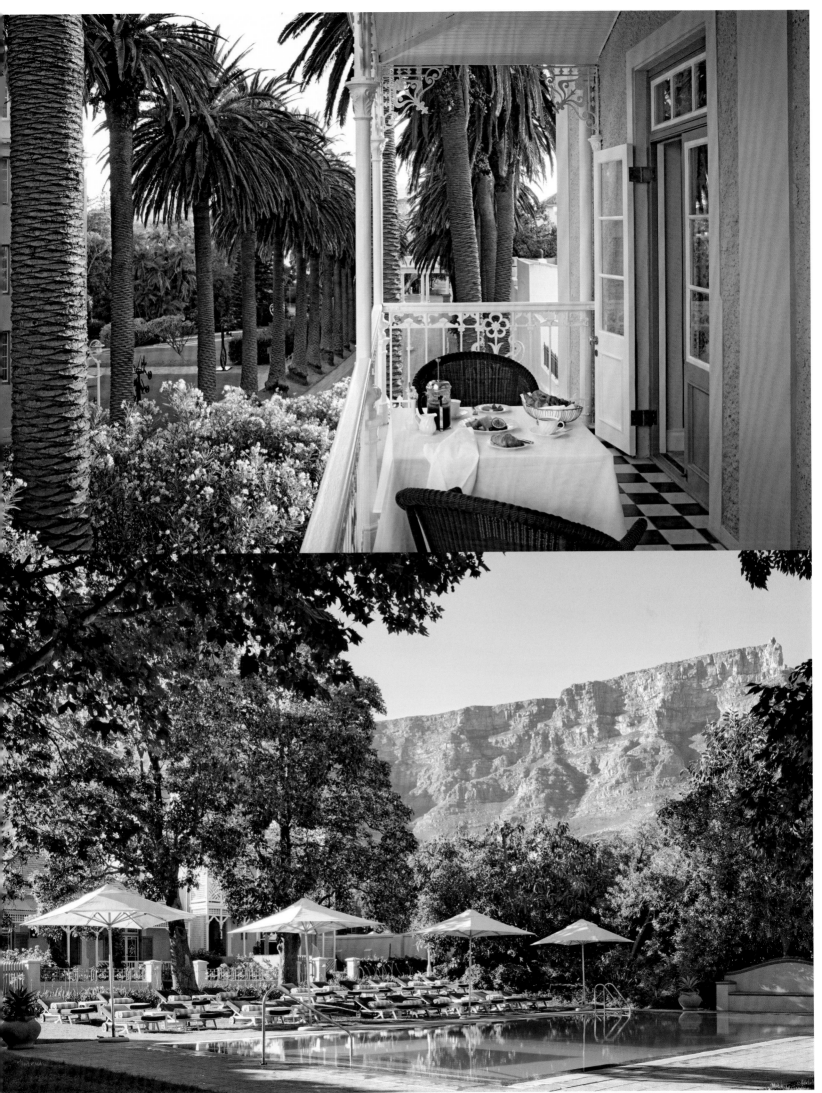

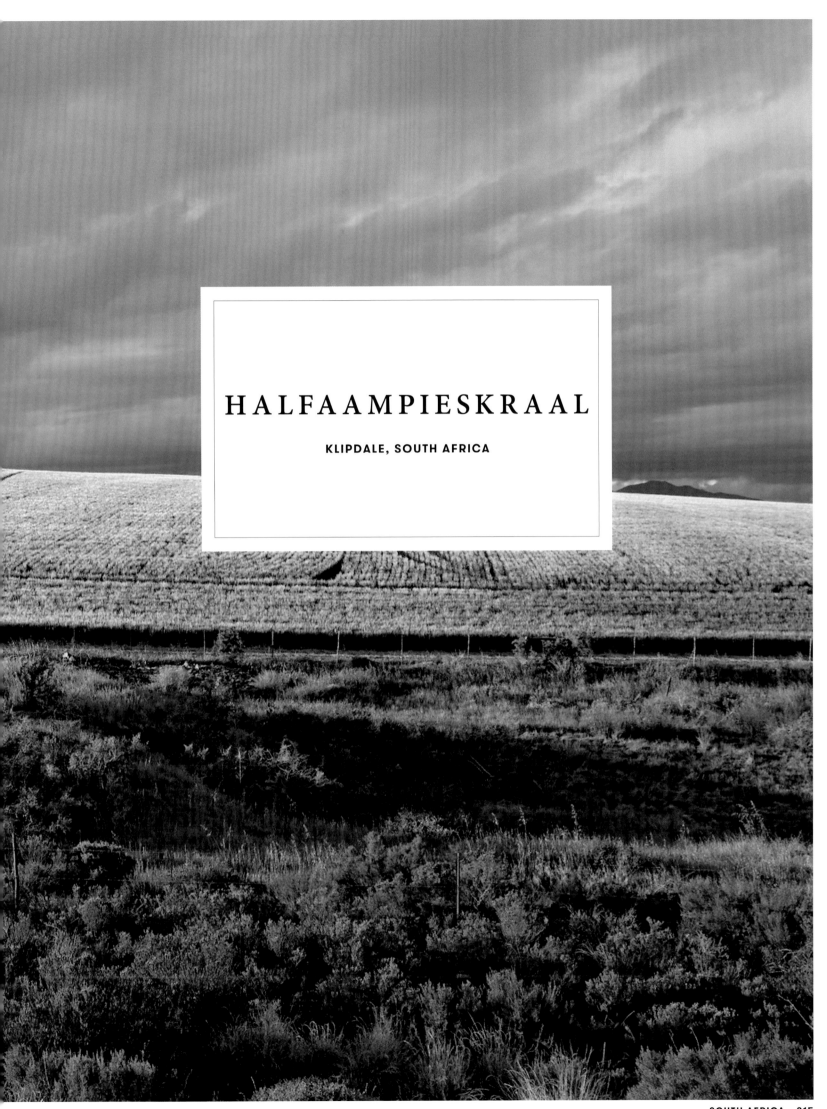

# HALFAAMPIESKRAAL

KLIPDALE, SOUTH AFRICA

# HALFAAMPIESKRAAL

P.O. Box 3, Klipdale 7288, South Africa
Tel. +27 82 569 0438 · rooms@kraal.biz
www.kraal.biz
*Open from the beginning of August until the end of June*

## LOVE OF THE LAND

At the heart of the Overberg region, South Africa presents its quiet, rustic face: if you travel from Cape Town, "over the mountain" (this is what the name means), you see fields where wheat and canola oil are grown, gently rolling hills and a seemingly infinite sky. This, for some 250 years, has set the scene for the Halfaampieskraal farm, on which Jan-Georg Solms grew up, now producing merino wool and featherdown for household use – and where he extends a warm welcome to visitors, for whom he has furnished five rooms in an outbuilding that once served as a school, stable and smithy. Behind thick masonry and beneath old wooden ceilings, these rooms with their whitewashed walls, black frames and simple furniture are slightly reminiscent of Greece, a country in which the owner loves to travel. Thanks to wonderfully large beds and modern bathrooms, the accommodation provides every amenity – while antiques and curiosities ensure it has charm and personality (and that guests do not really feel the lack of a television and minibar!).

In the main house, 50 meters away, are the lounges, library, bar and dining rooms, where hearty, down-to-earth meals are served in an opulent plantation ambience, with a stuffed peacock as a silent companion. The days pass around the pool, the evenings are spent by the open fire or in starlight – and nothing more is needed of Halfaampieskraal. It is the perfect spot for a break, a weekend … or longer. ◆ Book to pack: "The Way We Live" by Jan-Georg Solms and Ulrich Knoblauch – the farm's very own lifestyle and cookery book, available online or at local bookshops.

**DIRECTIONS** *160 km/100 miles east of Cape Town airport* · **RATES** *€€–€€€; including half board* · **ROOMS** *5 individually furnished rooms, all with a bathroom* · **FOOD** *Breakfast is served outdoors in summer. A wonderful three-course menu is served every evening* · **HISTORY** *The farm has been a guesthouse since 2006* · **X-FACTOR** *The loving attention to detail*

# LANDLIEBE

Im Herzen der Region Overberg zeigt sich Südafrika von seiner ruhigen, rustikalen Seite: Reist man von Kapstadt aus „über den Berg" (daher der Name der Gegend), fällt der Blick über Weizen- und Rapsfelder, auf sanft geschwungene Hügel und in einen scheinbar endlos weiten Himmel. Hier steht seit rund 250 Jahren der Hof Halfaampieskraal, auf dem Jan-Georg Solms aufwuchs. Er produziert Merinowolle sowie Daunen für den Eigenbedarf – und heißt auch Besucher herzlich willkommen. Für sie hat er in der ehemaligen Dependance, die einst als Schule, Stall und Schmiede diente, fünf Zimmer eingerichtet. Sie liegen hinter dicken Mauern und unter alten Holzdecken und erinnern mit ihren weiß getünchten Wänden, schwarzen Fensterrahmen und schlichten Möbeln ein bisschen an Griechenland, ein Lieblingsreiseland des Besitzers. Dank herrlich großer Betten und moderner Bäder bieten die Räume allen Komfort – Antiquitäten und Kuriositäten sorgen für Charme und Charakter (und dafür, dass man Fernseher und Minibar nicht wirklich vermisst!). Das 50 Meter entfernte Haupthaus beherbergt Lounges, Bibliothek, Bar und Esszimmer, wo in opulentem Plantagenambiente und mit einem ausgestopften Pfau als stillem Gast herzhafte Hausmannskost serviert wird. Tage, die am Pool dahinplätschern, und Abende am offenen Kamin oder im Sternenschein – mehr muss Halfaampieskraal gar nicht bieten. Es ist der perfekte Platz für eine Pause, für ein Wochenende … oder länger.
◆ Buchtipp: „The way we live" von Jan-Georg Solms und Ulrich Knoblauch, das hauseigene Lifestyle- und Kochbuch, kann man online oder im lokalen Buchhandel kaufen.

ANREISE *160 km östlich des Flughafens Kapstadt gelegen* · PREIS *€€–€€€; inklusive Halbpension* · ZIMMER *5 individuell eingerichtete Zimmer, alle mit Bad* · KÜCHE *Frühstück wird im Sommer im Freien serviert. Jeden Abend gibt es ein wunderbares 3-Gänge-Menü* · GESCHICHTE *Als Gasthaus dient der Hof seit 2006* · X-FAKTOR *Die Liebe zum Detail*

# LES NOURRITURES TERRESTRES

Au cœur de la région de l'Overberg, l'Afrique du Sud montre un visage calme et rustique : si vous venez du Cap et passez « au-dessus de la montagne » (d'où le nom de la région), vous verrez les champs de blé et de colza, des collines aux courbes douces et un ciel qui semble illimité. La ferme Halfaampieskraal existe depuis 250 ans environ ; Jan-Georg Solms qui a grandi ici, produit de la laine mérinos ainsi que du duvet pour ses besoins personnels, et accueille chaleureusement les visiteurs. Il a aménagé pour eux cinq chambres dans l'ancienne dépendance qui servait autrefois d'école, d'étable et de forge. Derrière des murs épais et sous de vieux plafonds en bois, leurs cloisons blanchies à la chaux, leurs encadrements noirs et leur mobilier sobre rappellent un peu la Grèce, une des destinations de vacances favorites du propriétaire. Avec leurs grands lits et leurs salles de bains modernes, les chambres offrent tout le confort – des antiquités et curiosités leur donnent du charme et de la personnalité (et font oublier l'absence de télévision et de minibar !). La maison principale, à 50 mètres, abrite des salons, une bibliothèque, un bar et des salles à manger, où une savoureuse cuisine maison est servie dans une ambiance de plantation opulente, sous le regard d'un paon empaillé. Des journées passées au bord de la piscine et des soirées au coin du feu ou à la lumière des étoiles – Halfaampieskraal n'a pas besoin d'offrir davantage. C'est l'endroit idéal pour se délasser le temps d'un week-end … ou plus. ◆ À lire : « Halfaampieskraal – The way we live » de Jan-Georg Solms et Ulrich Knoblauch. On peut acheter le livre de cuisine et lifestyle en ligne ou sur place dans les librairies.

ACCÈS *Situé à 160 km à l'est de l'aéroport du Cap* · PRIX *€€–€€€; demi-pension incluse* · CHAMBRES *5 chambres diversement meublées, toutes avec salle de bains* · RESTAURATION *L'été, le petit déjeuner est servi en plein air. On peut déguster tous les soirs un merveilleux menu de trois plats* · HISTOIRE *La ferme est utilisée comme auberge depuis 2006* · LES « PLUS » *L'amour du détail*

# OMAANDA LODGE

**ZANNIER RESERVE BY N/A'AN KU SÊ,
WINDHOEK EAST, NAMIBIA**

# OMAANDA LODGE

Farm no. 78, Rest of Ondekaremba Farm, Kapps Farm, Zannier Reserve by N/a'an ku sê, Windhoek East, Namibia
Tel. +264 81 145 5361 and +264 81 127 2425 · reservations@omaanda.com
www.zannierhotels.com

## ANGELINA'S AFRICA

Arnaud Zannier did not really have Namibia in mind when he was thinking about new locations for his exclusive hotels. But then he met Angelina Jolie, who was taking a holiday at his resort in Cambodia and enthused to him about a piece of land in Namibia – in a beautiful site in the savanna near Windhoek and adjacent to a reserve where friends of hers looked after injured or abandoned animals. Arnaud Zannier flew to Africa, bought the land, and in collaboration with his new neighbors and their foundation N/a'an ku sê ("God will protect us") established the 9,000-hectare Zannier Reserve, which is devoted to protecting endangered flora and fauna. Travelers can enjoy the unique natural surroundings and its rare inhabitants from close quarters – as guests at the luxurious Omaanda Lodge, which was built in the middle of the reserve and has a picture-postcard panorama across the wide plain to the mountains. Here visitors stay in thatched round huts, whose architecture is based on the traditional style of the Owambo and which

are fitted out in elegant earthy colors, with Namibian antiques and every imaginable amenity. Excursions are on offer twice a day, included in the room price and tailored to personal wishes. They range from an outdoor breakfast at dawn to a safari on the trail of elephants and giraffes, leopards and zebras. The service is rounded off by a spa where skin treatments using extracts from native herbs and spices are provided, an atmospheric restaurant and a "boma", an open-air hearth in typical African style.
◆ Book to pack: "The Heart of the Hunter" by Laurens van der Post.

DIRECTIONS *The Zannier Reserve lies on the Khomas Plateau. The Omaanda Lodge is 31 km/20 miles from Windhoek airport* · RATES *€€€€* · ROOMS *10 luxurious huts* · FOOD *Local products are made into a delicious meals by show cooks* · HISTORY *The Zannier Reserve was created in 2016. In July 2018 Omaanda was opened; further lodges are to follow* · X-FACTOR *Sustainable living in Namibia*

# ANGELINAS AFRIKA

Eigentlich hatte Arnaud Zannier Namibia gar nicht auf dem Radar, wenn er an neue Standorte für seine exklusiven Hotels dachte. Doch dann traf er Angelina Jolie, die in seinem Resort in Kambodscha Urlaub machte und ihm begeistert von einem Grundstück in Namibia erzählte – wunderschön in der Savanne bei Windhoek gelegen und an ein Reservat grenzend, in dem Freunde von ihr verletzte oder verlassene Wildtiere pflegten. Arnaud Zannier flog nach Afrika, kaufte das Land und schuf gemeinsam mit seinen neuen Nachbarn und deren Stiftung N/a'an ku sê ("Gott wird uns beschützen") das 9000 Hektar große Zannier-Reservat, das sich dem Schutz der bedrohten Flora und Fauna verschrieben hat. Reisende können die einzigartige Natur und ihre seltenen Bewohner aus nächster Nähe erleben – als Gäste der luxuriösen Lodge Omaanda, die mitten im Reservat entstand und ein Bilderbuchpanorama über die weite Ebene bis hin zu den Bergen eröffnet. Hier wohnt man in strohgedeckten Rundhütten, deren Architektur dem traditionellen Stil der Owambo nachempfunden ist und die in eleganten Erdtönen, mit namibischen Antiquitäten und allen erdenklichen Annehmlichkeiten ausgestattet sind. Zweimal täglich werden Ausflüge angeboten, die im Zimmerpreis enthalten sind und nach persönlichen Vorlieben maßgeschneidert werden – sie reichen vom Outdoor-Frühstück zu Sonnenaufgang bis zur Safari auf den Spuren von Elefanten und Giraffen, Leoparden und Zebras. Den Service komplett machen ein Spa, in dem die Haut mit Extrakten einheimischer Kräuter und Gewürze gepflegt wird, ein atmosphärisches Restaurant sowie eine „boma", die für Afrika typische Feuerstelle unter freiem Himmel. ◆ Buchtipp: „Das Herz des kleinen Jägers" von Laurens van der Post.

**ANREISE** *Das Zannier-Reservat liegt auf dem Khomas-Hochland-Plateau. Die Omaanda Lodge ist 31 km vom Flughafen Windhoek entfernt ·* **PREIS** *€€€€ ·* **ZIMMER** *10 luxuriöse Hütten ·* **KÜCHE** *Einheimische Produkte werden vor den Augen der Gäste köstlich zubereitet ·* **GESCHICHTE** *Das Zannier-Reservat entstand 2016. Im Juli 2018 wurde Omaanda eröffnet; weitere Lodges sollen folgen ·* **X-FAKTOR** *Hier erlebt man Namibia nachhaltig*

# L'AFRIQUE D'ANGELINA

En fait, Arnaud Zannier n'avait pas du tout songé à la Namibie lorsqu'il a pensé à de nouvelles destinations pour ses hôtels exclusifs. Et puis il a rencontré Angelina Jolie, en vacances dans son Resort au Cambodge, et qui lui a parlé avec enthousiasme d'un terrain en Namibie – magnifiquement situé dans la savane près de Windhoek et en bordure d'une réserve où ses amis soignaient des animaux blessés ou abandonnés. Arnaud Zannier s'est envolé pour l'Afrique, a acheté le terrain et, avec ses nouveaux voisins et leur fondation N/a'an ku sê (« Dieu nous protégera »), a créé la Réserve de Zannier, d'une superficie de 9 000 hectares, consacrée à la protection de la faune et de la flore menacées. Les voyageurs peuvent découvrir de près la nature unique et ses habitants rares – en tant qu'hôtes du luxueux Omaanda Lodge, qui a été construit au milieu de la réserve et ouvre un panorama digne d'un livre d'images sur la vaste plaine et les montagnes. Vous y vivrez dans des cabanes rondes au toit de chaume, dont l'architecture est inspirée du style traditionnel Owambo et qui sont meublées dans des tons de terre élégants, avec des antiquités namibiennes et tout le confort imaginable. Deux fois par jour, des excursions sont proposées, incluses dans le prix de la chambre et adaptées aux préférences personnelles – du petit déjeuner en plein air au lever du soleil aux safaris sur les traces des éléphants et des girafes, des léopards et des zèbres. Un spa, avec des soins à base d'extraits d'herbes et d'épices de la région, un restaurant à l'ambiance chaleureuse ainsi qu'un « boma », le feu à ciel ouvert typiquement africain, complètent l'ensemble. ◆ À lire : « Le Monde perdu du Kalahari » de Laurens van der Post.

**ACCÈS** *La Réserve Zannier est située sur le plateau de Khomas Hochland. L'Omaanda Lodge est à 31 km de l'aéroport de Windhoek ·* **PRIX** *€€€€ ·* **CHAMBRES** *10 cabanes de luxe ·* **RESTAURATION** *Des plats savoureux à base de produits locaux sont préparés sous vos yeux ·* **HISTOIRE** *La Réserve Zannier a vu le jour en 2016. Omaanda a ouvert ses portes en juillet 2018 ; d'autres lodges doivent suivre ·* **LES « PLUS »** *La Namibie sous son aspect « tourisme durable »*

# HOANIB SKELETON COAST CAMP

**SKELETON COAST, KAOKOVELD, NAMIBIA**

# HOANIB SKELETON COAST CAMP

Skeleton Coast, Kaokoveld, Namibia
Tel. +27 11 257 50 00 · enquiry@wilderness.co.za
www.wilderness-safaris.com

## IN THE MIDDLE OF NOWHERE

The Kaokoveld in the north-west of Namibia could easily be the backdrop for a science-fiction film: dramatically rugged rocks, dried-out river beds, gravelly plains of scrub and bush – an almost unreal-looking landscape in shades of brown, above which the steel-blue color of the arching sky is such that you can practically see the heat. This is the site of the Hoanib Skeleton Coast Camp, which is adapted to the extreme conditions of the desert as if this were a matter of course, the color and shape of its curving tent roofs being reminiscent of dunes. Made from canvas with protection against ultra-violet rays, they provide much-needed shade. Moreover, the tents were erected on raised slabs of cement, beneath which a cooling breeze can blow. The interiors, too, take up the colors of nature. The designer Sharon Milstead has harmoniously composed furniture and fabrics in white, beige and pale blue, elegantly combining them with African accessories, all luxuriously complemented with private bathrooms each with a toilet and running water. The tent village also has a central area with a restaurant, an open-air hearth and even a small pool. The camp is an ideal base for setting out on safaris – elephants and lions, hyenas and giraffes live in the desert – or for picnics in hidden oases and a trip to Namibia's legendary Skeleton Coast, regarded as the world's largest cemetery for ships, but also home to a famous colony of seals. ◆ Book to pack: "Namibian Nights" by Michelle van Hoop.

**DIRECTIONS** *On private property in the Namib Desert, accessible only by light aircraft (from the Doro Nawas airstrip, which has connections to Windhoek and Swakopmund)* · **RATES** *€€€€; all inclusive* · **ROOMS** *8 luxury tents, including 1 family tent* · **FOOD** *In the main tent an excellent breakfast, lunch and dinner are served* · **HISTORY** *Opened in August 2014* · **X-FACTOR** *The construction of the camp, which is powered 100 per cent by solar energy, was as environmentally friendly as possible*

# MITTEN IM NIRGENDWO

Das Kaokoveld im Nordwesten Namibias könnte ohne Weiteres als Kulisse für einen Science-Fiction-Film dienen: Dramatisch zerklüftete Felsen, ausgedorrte Flussbetten, Kiesebenen mit struppigem Buschwerk – eine beinahe unwirklich erscheinende Szenerie in Braunnuancen, über der sich ein derart stahlblauer Himmel spannt, dass man die Hitze fast sehen kann. Hier steht das Hoanib Skeleton Coast Camp, das sich den Extrembedingungen der Wüste wie selbstverständlich anpasst: Seine geschwungenen aus Segeltuch gefertigten Zeltdächer mit UV-Schutz erinnern in Farbe und Form an Dünen und spenden wertvollen Schatten. Zudem wurden die Zelte auf erhöhten Zementplatten errichtet, unter denen eine kühlende Brise durchziehen kann. Auch das Interieur greift die Töne der Natur wieder auf. Designerin Sharon Milstead hat Möbel und Stoffe in Weiß, Beige sowie Hellblau harmonisch zusammengestellt, mit afrikanischen Accessoires elegant kombiniert und mit privaten Bädern samt Toilette und fließendem Wasser ausgestattet. Zur Zeltstadt gehört zudem ein Hauptbereich mit Restaurant, Feuerstelle unter freiem Himmel und sogar einem kleinen Pool. Das Camp ist ein idealer Ausgangspunkt für Safaris – in der Wüste leben Elefanten und Löwen, Hyänen und Giraffen –, für Picknicks an versteckten Oasen und für einen Ausflug an Namibias legendäre Skelettküste, die als einer der größten Schiffsfriedhöfe der Welt gilt, aber auch eine berühmte Robbenkolonie beheimatet. ◆ Buchtipp: „Namibische Nächte" von Michelle van Hoop.

*ANREISE Auf einem Privatgelände in der Namibwüste gelegen und nur per Leichtflugzeug zu erreichen (ab dem Doro Nawas Airstrip, zu dem Verbindungen ab Windhoek und Swakopmund bestehen) · PREIS €€€€; all-inclusive · ZIMMER 8 Luxuszelte, darunter 1 Familienzelt · KÜCHE Im Hauptzelt werden sehr gutes Frühstück, Mittag- und Abendessen serviert · GESCHICHTE Im August 2014 eröffnet · X-FAKTOR Das Camp wurde so umweltschonend wie möglich gebaut und wird zu 100 Prozent mit Solarstrom betrieben*

# AU MILIEU DE NULLE PART

Situé dans le nord-ouest de la Namibie, le Kaokoveld pourrait facilement servir de décor à un film de science-fiction : des rochers déchiquetés, des lits de rivière asséchés, des plaines de gravier garnies de buissons hirsutes – un paysage presque irréel dans des nuances de brun, et, au-dessus de tout cela, un ciel si bleu que l'on croit voir la chaleur vibrer. Ici se dresse le Hoanib Skeleton Coast Camp, parfaitement adapté aux conditions extrêmes du désert : ses toits de tente incurvés en toile avec protection UV évoquent les dunes de par leur couleur et leur forme et offrent une ombre précieuse. De plus, les tentes ont été montées sur des dalles de ciment surélevées sous lesquelles peut passer une brise rafraîchissante. L'intérieur reprend également des couleurs de la nature. La décoratrice Sharon Milstead a marié harmonieusement meubles et tissus dans des tons de blanc, beige et bleu clair, les a combinés élégamment avec des accessoires africains et les a luxueusement complétés avec des salles de bains privées avec toilettes et eau courante. Le village de tentes dispose également d'un espace principal avec restaurant, foyer en plein air et même une petite piscine. Le camp est un point de départ idéal pour les safaris – éléphants et lions, hyènes et girafes vivent dans le désert –, pour pique-niquer dans des oasis cachées et pour explorer la légendaire côte des Squelettes de Namibie, considérée comme l'un des plus grands cimetières d'épaves de bateaux au monde, mais qui abrite aussi une célèbre colonie de phoques. ◆ À lire : « Cartographie de l'oubli » de Niels Labuzan.

*ACCÈS Situé sur un terrain privé dans le désert de Namibie et uniquement accessible par un petit avion (au départ de Doro Nawas Airstrip ; il existe aussi des liaisons au départ de Windhoek et Swakopmund) · PRIX €€€€; tout compris · CHAMBRES 8 tentes de luxe dont une tente familiale · RESTAURATION Un excellent petit déjeuner, le déjeuner et le dîner sont servis dans la tente principale · HISTOIRE Ouvert depuis août 2014 · LES « PLUS » Le camp a été construit dans le plus grand respect possible de l'environnement et fonctionne 100 pour cent à l'énergie solaire*

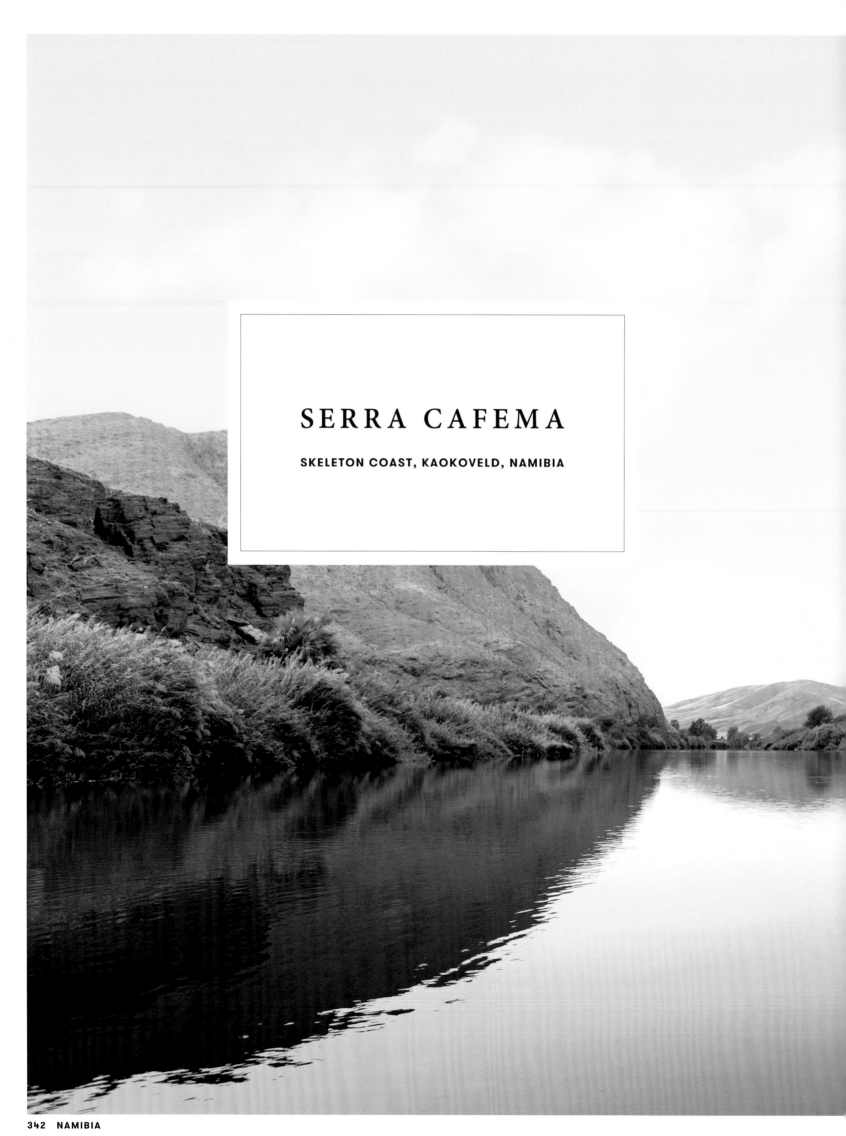

# SERRA CAFEMA

### SKELETON COAST, KAOKOVELD, NAMIBIA

# SERRA CAFEMA

Skeleton Coast, Kaokoveld, Namibia
Tel. +27 11 257 50 00 · enquiry@wilderness.co.za
www.wilderness-safaris.com

## A GUEST OF THE HIMBA

The country on the Kunene River is the land of the Himba, one of the last semi-nomadic peoples in Namibia. Since time immemorial the Himba have been known for their pride and friendliness, their skill as stockbreeders and farmers, and for the beauty rituals of their women, who protect their faces from the sun with a red paste, have elaborate hairstyles and wear heavy jewelry. If Himba are in the area, guests at this lodge have the rare opportunity to visit their villages and to learn more about their lives and history. Serra Cafema, idyllically sited beneath gnarled trees on the banks of the Kunene, has also taken many Himba traditions as its model. The main area of the premises, for example, was built in the manner of a Himba village, with the buildings linked together through external areas. The covers for menus and wine lists are made from thick, ochre-colored leather and in cooperation with Himba women, a local company have developed a series of care products using plants such as the fragrant Namibian myrrh. The chalets at the lodge, built from stone, wood and thatch, are decorated with outsized portraits of the Himba. The beautiful accommodation is also equipped with extra-large beds, indoor and outdoor bathrooms, floor-to-ceiling windows and private terraces from which guests can look out over the river to hear the gentle lapping of water. A safari holiday can hardly be more peaceful and enjoyable!
◆ Book to pack: "Daniel" by Henning Mankell.

DIRECTIONS *One of the remotest camps in Namibia – in the far north of the country in the Hartmann Valley. Serra Cafema has its own airstrip for light aircraft (connections e.g. from Windhoek and Doro Nawas)* · RATES *€€€€, all inclusive* · ROOMS *18 luxurious chalets, including one for families* · FOOD *A successful combination of traditional and modern Namibian food. Vegetarians, too, are catered for* · HISTORY *The lodge was founded in 2003 and reopened in 2018 following renovation* · X-FACTOR *A walk in the dunes with picture-postcard views of the region*

# ZU GAST BEI DEN HIMBA

Das Land am Kunene-Fluss ist das Land der Himba, eines der letzten Halbnomandenvölker in Namibia. Seit jeher sind die Himba für ihren Stolz und ihre Freundlichkeit, ihr Geschick als Viehzüchter und Bauern sowie die Schönheitsrituale ihrer Frauen bekannt, die ihr Gesicht mit einer roten Paste vor der Sonne schützen sowie kunstvolle Frisuren und schweren Schmuck tragen. Sind die Himba in der Nähe, haben Gäste dieser Lodge die Gelegenheit, ihre Dörfer zu besuchen und mehr über ihre Geschichte und ihr Leben zu erfahren. Serra Cafema, idyllisch unter knorrigen Bäumen am Ufer des Kunene gelegen, hat sich zudem zahlreiche Himba-Traditionen zum Vorbild genommen: So ist der Hauptbereich der Anlage nach Art eines Himba-Dorfes konstruiert, in dem die Gebäude durch Außenbereiche miteinander verbunden sind. Die Hüllen für Menü- und Weinkarten wurden aus dickem, ockerfarbenem Leder gefertigt, dem Lieblingsmaterial des Volkes. Und gemeinsam mit Himbafrauen entwickelte ein lokales Unternehmen eine Serie von Badprodukten mit pflanzlichen Wirkstoffen wie der duftenden namibischen Myrrhe. Die Chalets der Lodge, erbaut aus Stein, Holz und Stroh, schmücken überdimensionale Porträts der Himba. Zudem bieten die schönen Unterkünfte extragroße Betten, Innen- und Außenbäder sowie raumhohe Fensterfronten und private Terrassen, von denen man auf den Fluss schaut und dem leisen Plätschern des Wassers lauscht. So ruhig und genussvoll kann Safariurlaub sein! ◆ Buchtipp: „Die rote Antilope" von Henning Mankell.

**ANREISE** *Eines der abgelegensten Camps in Namibia – im äußersten Norden des Landes im Hartmann-Tal errichtet. Serra Cafema besitzt eine eigene Landebahn für Leichtflugzeuge (Verbindungen z. B. ab Windhoek und Doro Nawas)* · **PREIS** *€€€€; all-inclusive* · **ZIMMER** *8 luxuriöse Chalets, darunter eines für Familien* · **KÜCHE** *Eine gelungene Verbindung von traditioneller und moderner namibischer Küche. Auch für Vegetarier wird gut gesorgt* · **GESCHICHTE** *Gegründet 2003, die Lodge wurde 2018 nach einer Renovierung neu eröffnet* · **X-FAKTOR** *Eine Dünenwanderung mit Bilderbuchblicken über die Region*

# INVITÉ CHEZ LES HIMBA

Le fleuve Kunene arrose la terre des Himba, l'un des derniers peuples semi-nomades de Namibie. Depuis toujours les Himba sont réputés pour leur fierté et leur gentillesse, leur talent d'éleveurs et d'agriculteurs, sans oublier les rituels de beauté de leurs épouses, qui protègent leur visage du soleil avec une pâte rouge, portent des coiffures artistiques et des bijoux opulents. Si les Himba sont à proximité, les hôtes de ce lodge peuvent exceptionnellement visiter leurs villages et en apprendre davantage sur leur histoire et leur vie. Le Serra Cafema, idéalement situé à l'ombre d'arbres noueux sur les rives du Kunene, s'inspire en outre de nombreuses traditions Himba : la partie principale du complexe est construite dans le style d'un village Himba, dans lequel les bâtiments sont reliés par des espaces extérieurs. Les couvertures des menus et des cartes des vins sont en cuir ocre épais, la matière préférée du peuple Himba. Et, en collaboration avec les femmes, une entreprise locale a développé une série de produits pour le bain à base de principes actifs végétaux tels que la myrrhe parfumée de Namibie. Les chalets du lodge, construits en pierre, en bois et en paille, sont ornés de portraits surdimensionnés des Himba – les magnifiques hébergements offrent également des lits extra-larges, des bains intérieurs et extérieurs, des baies vitrées à hauteur de plafond et des terrasses privées d'où l'on peut regarder la rivière et écouter le doux clapotement de l'eau. On voit que les vacances en safari peuvent être tranquilles et plaisantes ! ◆ À lire : « Le fils du vent » de Henning Mankell.

**ACCÈS** *Situé à l'extrême nord du pays dans la vallée de Hartmann, c'est l'un des camps les plus isolés de Namibie. Serra Cafema possède une piste pour les petits avions (par exemple liaisons au départ de Windhoek et Doro Nawas)* · **PRIX** *€€€€; tout compris* · **CHAMBRES** *8 chalets luxueux, dont un réservé aux familles* · **RESTAURATION** *Un mariage réussi de cuisine namibienne traditionnelle et moderne. Les végétariens s'y régaleront aussi* · **HISTOIRE** *Créé en 2003, le lodge a été réouvert en 2018 après des rénovations* · **LES « PLUS »** *Une randonnée à travers les dunes avec des vues exceptionnelles sur la région*

# KULALA
# DESERT LODGE

SOSSUSVLEI, NAMIBIA

# KULALA DESERT LODGE

Sossusvlei, Namibia
Tel. +27 11 257 50 00 · enquiry@wilderness.co.za
www.wilderness-safaris.com

## A LEGENDARY LANDSCAPE

Here, at the foot of the red dunes of Sossusvlei, there was once just a cattle and sheep farm – until the land was sold in the mid-1990s and the private Kulala Reserve established. In the meantime, this terrain has regenerated its ecosystem, and native animals such as the gemsbock, fox, jackal and hyena have returned to these 27,000 hectares of desert. The heart of the reserve is this lodge with 23 kulalas ("kulala" being the Oshiwambo word for "sleep"), rustic huts equipped simply with a bed and bathroom. At the rear, stands a roof terrace on which guests can spend the night beneath the open sky – if counting the stars does not keep them awake. By day, everything revolves around the wonderful views: on walks and tours by jeep or e-bike, guests explore the spectacular sand dunes, up to 400 meters high, which have evolved over millions of years. For an additional price, trips in hot-air balloons are on offer, and to admire this legendary landscape from the air is a unique experience. As it can get extremely hot in the daytime, early morning is the best time for excursions. The late afternoon, when the temperatures fall, is reserved for a sundowner safari: after a drive through the reserve, guests enjoy a drink at a spot with a panorama and see the most beautiful sunset imaginable. ◆ Book to pack: "The Other Side of Silence" by André Brink.

**DIRECTIONS** *Kulala is the lodge closest to the dunes and has a private entrance to the Namib Naukluft National Park; this saves valuable time when visiting. Windhoek is 340 km/210 miles away* · **RATES** *€€€€; all inclusive. Only balloon trips are charged separately* · **ROOMS** *23 huts made from earth, wood, canvas and thatch* · **FOOD** *A sumptuous breakfast buffet and fresh Namibian menus for lunch and dinner, changing daily* · **HISTORY** *The reserve was founded in 1996, the lodge two years later* · **X-FACTOR** *From the shared terrace there is a view of a waterhole and, with a little luck, animals drinking there*

## EINE LEGENDÄRE LANDSCHAFT

Früher gab es hier, am Fuß der roten Dünen von Sossusvlei, nur eine Rinder- und Schaffarm, bis das Grundstück Mitte der 1990er Jahre verkauft wurde und das private Kulala-Reservat entstand. Inzwischen hat sich wieder ein eigenes Ökosystem etabliert, und auf das 27.000 Hektar große Wüstengelände sind einheimische Tiere wie Gemsböcke, Füchse, Schakale sowie Hyänen zurückgekehrt. Herzstück des Reservats ist diese Lodge mit 23 Kulalas („kulala" bedeutet auf Oshiwambo „schlafen") – rustikalen Hütten, die innen schlicht mit Bett und Bad ausgestattet sind. Draußen, auf der Rückseite des Häuschens, besitzen sie eine kleine Dachterrasse, auf der man unter freiem Himmel übernachten kann, sofern einen das Sternezählen nicht vom Schlafen abhält. Um traumhafte Ausblicke dreht sich auch tagsüber alles: Bei Wanderungen und Touren mit dem Jeep oder E-Bike entdecken die Gäste die spektakulären, bis zu 400 Meter hohen Sanddünen, die im Lauf von Millionen von Jahren entstanden sind. Gegen Aufpreis werden zudem Fahrten im Heißluftballon angeboten – diese legendäre Landschaft aus der Luft zu bewundern, ist ein einzigartiges Erlebnis. Da es tagsüber extrem heiß werden kann, ist der frühe Morgen die beste Zeit für Ausflüge. Der späte Nachmittag, wenn die Temperaturen sinken, bleibt für eine Sundowner-Safari reserviert: Nach einer Fahrt durchs Reservat genießt man an einem Panoramaplatz einen Drink und den schönsten Sonnenuntergang, den man sich vorstellen kann.
◆ Buchtipp: „Die andere Seite der Stille" von André Brink.

**ANREISE** *Kulala ist die den Dünen am nächsten gelegene Lodge und hat einen privaten Eingang zum Namib-Naukluft National Park; das spart wertvolle Zeit beim Besuch. Windhoek ist 340 km entfernt ·* **PREIS** *€€€€; all-inclusive. Nur Ballonfahrten werden separat berechnet ·* **ZIMMER** *23 Hütten aus Lehm, Holz, Segeltuch und Stroh ·* **KÜCHE** *Üppiges Frühstücksbüfett und frische, täglich wechselnde namibische Menüs am Mittag und Abend ·* **GESCHICHTE** *Das Reservat wurde 1996 gegründet, die Lodge zwei Jahre später ·* **X-FAKTOR** *Von der Gemeinschaftsterrasse aus blickt man auf ein Wasserloch und kann mit etwas Glück Tiere beim Trinken beobachten*

## UN PAYSAGE MYTHIQUE

Il n'y avait autrefois qu'une seule exploitation bovine et ovine au pied des dunes rouges de Sossusvlei – et puis les terres ont été vendues au milieu des années 1990 et la réserve privée de Kulala a été créée. Entre-temps, un écosystème s'est établi et des animaux comme les gemsboks, les renards, les chacals et les hyènes sont revenus dans cette zone désertique de 27 000 hectares. Le cœur de la réserve est ce lodge qui abrite 23 kulalas (« kulala » signifie « dormir » dans la langue oshiwambo) – des cabanes rustiques, n'abritant qu'un lit et une salle de bains. Dehors, à l'arrière, une petite terrasse sur le toit invite à passer la nuit à l'air libre, si tant est que compter les étoiles ne vous empêche pas de dormir. Pendant la journée, il n'est question aussi que de panoramas fantastiques : lors de randonnées et de tours en jeep ou en vélo électrique, les visiteurs découvrent les spectaculaires dunes de sable, créées au cours de millions d'années, et qui peuvent atteindre 400 m de haut. Des tours en montgolfière sont également possibles moyennant supplément – admirer du ciel ce paysage mythique est une expérience inoubliable. Comme il peut faire extrêmement chaud pendant la journée, il vaut mieux partir en excursion tôt le matin. La fin de l'après-midi, lorsque les températures chutent, est réservée au « safari-coucher de soleil » : après avoir traversé la réserve en voiture, vous vous arrêterez dans un site panoramique, et observerez le plus beau coucher de soleil que vous puissiez imaginer en sirotant un drink. ◆ À lire : « Au-delà du silence » d'André Brink.

**ACCÈS** *Kulala est le lodge le plus proche des dunes avec un accès privé au parc national Namib-Naukluft, ce qui fait gagner un temps précieux. Windhoek est situé à 340 km ·* **PRIX** *€€€€; tout compris. Seuls les vols en montgolfière sont facturés en sus ·* **CHAMBRES** *23 cabanes en argile, bois, toile et paille ·* **RESTAURATION** *Un buffet opulent au petit déjeuner. Des plats de la cuisine namibienne aux produits frais avec des menus renouvelés chaque jour sont proposés le midi et le soir ·* **HISTOIRE** *La réserve a été créée en 1996, le lodge deux ans plus tard ·* **LES « PLUS »** *Un point d'eau est bien visible de la terrasse commune. Avec un peu de chance, on peut observer les animaux en train de s'abreuver*

# PHOTO CREDITS

8 **Nord-Pinus Tanger**
Thierry Arensma

16 **Numa Marrakech**
Gianni Basso/Vega MG

30 **Amanjena**
René Stoeltie

38 **Berber Lodge**
Cecile Perrinet Lhermitte

50 **Scarabeo Camp**
pp. 50–52, 55 bottom, 56–57, 59
Sophia van den Hoek; p. 55 top
Sven Laurent; p. 58 Nelly Siby

60 **Orient Desert Camp**
Gianni Basso/Vega MG

70 **Adrère Amellal Eco Lodge**
Deidi von Schaewen

78 **Hotel Marsam**
pp. 78–79, 83 Mireille Roobaert;
p. 80 Ricardo Labougle/Hugo Curletto

84 **Hotel Al Moudira**
pp. 84–86, 89 bottom, 90–93
Dylan Chandler; p. 89 top
Deidi von Schaewen

94 **One & Only Nyungwe House**
Ruppert, supplied by the hotel

102 **Magashi**
Dana Allen/Wilderness Safaris

110 **Bisate Lodge**
Wilderness Safaris, pp. 110–111,
115 top, 117 David Crookes; pp. 112,
115 bottom, 116, 118–119 Dana Allen

120 **Sanctuary Gorilla Forest Camp**
Supplied by the hotel

126 **Sarara Camp**
Supplied by the hotel

132 **Arijiju**
pp. 132–134, 137–138, 141 top,
142, 143 bottom Crookes & Jackson;
pp. 139–140, 141 bottom, 143 top Dook

144 **Dodo's Tower**
Supplied by the hotel

150 **Hippo Point**
Deidi von Schaewen

156 **The Giraffe Manor**
pp. 156–157, 158 Robin Moore;
p. 161 supplied by the hotel

162 **Cottar's 1920s Safari Camp**
Supplied by the hotel

168 **Peponi Hotel**
pp. 168–169, 170, 173 bottom
supplied by the hotel; p. 173 top
Carol Korschen, DePonte
Photography

174 **Kinondo Kwetu**
Dan Kullberg/Kinondo Kwetu

182 **Chumbe Island Coral Park**
pp. 182–183, 187 top, 189 Markus
Meissl; pp. 184, 187 bottom, 188
Deidi von Schaewen

190 **Gibb's Farm**
p. 190–192, 195 bottom, 196–197
supplied by the hotel; pp. 195 top,
198–199 Scott Ramsay

200 **Tarangire Treetops**
Silverless, supplied by the hotel

206 **Serengeti Safari Camp**
nomad-tanzania.com

214 **Fregate Island Private**
Supplied by the hotel

220 **Constance Tsarabanjina**
Supplied by the hotel

226 **Bazaruto Island Resort**
Paul Changuion/WildWeb

232 **Sausage Tree Camp**
Supplied by the hotel

240 **Sandibe Okavango Safari Lodge**
pp. 240–242, 245, 359
supplied by andBeyond

246 **Nxabega Okavango Tented Camp**
Supplied by andBeyond

254 **Mombo Camp**
Crookes & Jackson/Wilderness Safaris

260 **Garonga Safari Camp**
Bernie Smith, supplied by the hotel

270 **Singita Boulders Lodge**
Supplied by the hotel

276 **Ulusaba**
p. 276–279, 280 top Ulusaba/Virgin
Limited Edition; pp. 278, 280 bottom,
283 bottom supplied by the hotel

284 **Le Quartier Français**
Supplied by the hotel

290 **Babylonstoren**
Supplied by the hotel

306 **Mount Nelson Hotel**
Supplied by the hotel

314 **Halfaampieskraal**
Ulrich Knoblauch

324 **Omaanda Lodge**
Karel Balas/Vega MG

334 **Hoanib Skeleton Coast Camp**
Wilderness Safaris, pp. 334–336,
339–341 bottom Dana Allen;
pp. 341 top Olwen Evans

342 **Serra Cafema**
Wilderness Safaris, pp. 342–343,
347, 348 bottom, 349 top Tegan
Cunniffe; pp. 344, 348 top, 349
bottom Dana Allen

350 **Kulala Desert Lodge**
Wilderness Safaris, p. 350–351
Mary-Anne Van Der Byl; p. 352,
355, 356 top, 357 Dana Allen;
p. 356 bottom Daniel Myberg

# IMPRINT

**EDITING, ART DIRECTION AND LAYOUT**
Angelika Taschen, Berlin

**PROJECT MANAGER**
Stephanie Paas, Cologne

**DESIGN**
Maximiliane Hüls, Cologne

**TEXTS**
Christiane Reiter, Brussels

**GERMAN TRANSLATION**
Sylvia Still for LocTeam, S.L., Barcelona;
Birgit Lamerz-Beckschäfer, Datteln

**ENGLISH TRANSLATION**
John Sykes, Cologne

**FRENCH TRANSLATION**
Stéphanie Tabone for LocTeam, S.L., Barcelona;
Alice Pétillot, Paris;
Michèle Schreyer, Cologne

**EACH AND EVERY TASCHEN BOOK PLANTS A SEED!**
TASCHEN is a carbon-neutral publisher. Each year, we offset our annual carbon emissions with carbon credits at the Instituto Terra, a reforestation program in Minas Gerais, Brazil, founded by Lélia and Sebastião Salgado. To find out more about this ecological partnership, please check: www.taschen.com/zerocarbon
**Inspiration: unlimited. Carbon footprint: zero.**

To stay informed about TASCHEN and our upcoming titles, please subscribe to our free magazine at www.taschen.com/magazine, follow us on Instagram and Facebook, or e-mail your questions to contact@taschen.com.

The published information, addresses and pictures have been researched with the utmost care. However, no responsibility or liability can be taken for the correctness of details.

Printed in Slovakia
ISBN 978-3-8365-7813-4

**FRONT COVER**
Garonga Safari Camp, South Africa. Photo: Paul Changuion/WildWeb

**BACK COVER**
Scarabeo, Morocco. Photo: Nelly Siby, supplied by the hotel

**ENDPAPERS**
Scarabeo, Morocco. Photo: Sophia van den Hoek, supplied by the hotel

**PRICE CATEGORIES**
€ up to 150 € · €€ up to 250 € ·
€€€ up to 450 € · €€€€ over 450 €